5-2-12

Great Dog Stories

M.R. Wells Kris Young
Connie Fleishauer

D1166411

HARVEST HOUSE PUBLISHERS

EUGENE, OREGON

Cover by Left Coast Design, Portland, Oregon

Cover photo © Eric Isselée / Shutterstock

Published in association with the literary agency of Mark Sweeney & Associates, Bonita Springs, FL 34135.

The information shared by the authors is from their personal experience and should not be considered professional advice. Readers should consult their own dog care professionals regarding issues related to the health, safety, grooming, and training of their pets.

In some cases, names and minor details of stories may have been changed to protect privacy.

GREAT DOG STORIES
Copyright © 2012 by M.R. Wells, Kris Young, and Connie Fleishauer
Published by Harvest House Publishers
Eugene, Oregon 97402
www.harvesthousepublishers.com

Library of Congress Cataloging-in-Publication Data
    Wells, M. R. (Marion R.), 1948-
    Great dog stories / M.R. Wells, Kris Young, and Connie Fleishauer.
        p. cm.
    ISBN 978-0-7369-2882-3 (pbk.)
    ISBN 978-0-7369-4239-3 (eBook)
    1. Dog owners—Prayers and devotions. I. Young, Kris, 1953- II. Fleishauer, Connie. III. Title.
    BV4596.A54W452 2012
    242—dc23

                                                                 2011016828

Printed in the United States of America

          12 13 14 15 16 17 18 19 20 / VP-SK / 10 9 8 7 6 5 4 3 2 1

*We joyfully dedicate this book
to the great dogs and people in our lives,
and to our infinitely greater God,
who made us all.*

It Takes a "Pack" to Write a Book

How fitting that the dogs we love are pack animals. We are too. This book would never have been birthed otherwise. Thanks to all who lent a paw by sharing their stories or praying for us. Thanks to our agents, Mark and Janet Sweeney, who shared our vision and helped make it come true. Special thanks to Nicole Overbey, DVM, for giving our manuscript a top-notch veterinary checkup. And huge gratitude to our amazing team at Harvest House Publishers! You win best in show, and we are so blessed to have you!

Most of all, we are eternally grateful to our awesome God, who gave us dogs and stories and invites us into His!

Contents

Part I
Tales to Tug Your Heart

Part II
Tales to Stretch Your Faith

Part III
Tales to Light Your Path

Part IV
Tales to Lift Your Spirits

The Dog Who Amazes

There is a certain instinctive fellowship among dog lovers. It's like proud parents getting together. We grab our cell phones and click through our photos to share their latest mug shots. We trade stories about the endearing and often amazing things they've done. We marvel at their loyalty and love.

A lucky few, like this book's authors, have the privilege of going one "paw" further. We are blessed to collect their antics into books. And in the midst of being blown away by our beloved canine friends, we are even more blown away by the God who made them.

Dogs aren't just an accident of nature. They are a grand design and a gift from our loving Lord. He knew what dogs and humans could give to each other. He knew we needed their furry comfort in our frenetic twenty-first-century world. And in a society where dogs are far more common than sheep, He knew He could use them as pointers and pictures to draw us closer to Him.

Without "pulling you by the tale," we hope the stories in this book will not only entertain and amuse you, but offer some spiritual kibble to gnaw on. We hope they'll give you new insights— some we didn't even catch ourselves. And we hope they will spur you to look with new eyes at the dogs in your life for the messages God may be sending through them to your heart.

Meet the Authors' Pups

 **Becca Wells** is a gorgeous reddish-tan and white Pomeranian princess. She has a huge heart in her petite little body. When I'm hurting, she leaps into my lap and lavishes me with doggie kisses.

 **Marley Wells** is a handsome white-and-sable papillon mix. With his markings, this six-pounder makes me think of a tiny paint horse. He loves snuggling and cuddling with me, pulling his doggie sister's tail, and trying to convince my other four-foots he's "top dog."

 **Morgan Wells** was part Sheltie, part "potluck," and all personality. He grabbed my heart when I got him as a two-year-old rescue, and held it in his gentle paws ever after.

 **Munchie Wells** is a stunning tricolored papillon mix. This lover dog is mellow most of the time. But every now and then, he'll push past his doggie and kitty siblings, squeeze close to me or climb into my lap, and paw at me as if to say, "You're mine!"

McPherson Fleishauer was a beautiful and loving shepherd mix. He was our first pup as a young married couple, and we all learned a lot together. He matured into a fine working farm dog and served as a canine nanny to all three of our children when they were little. Even in old age, he never relinquished his role as our family's friend and protector.

Stuart Fleishauer is a handsome tan and white Welsh corgi. He is strong and active, but acts like a gentleman—um, "gentledog"—with his canine sister, Squitchey. He loves being with us—protecting, cuddling, and licking our ears.

Squitchey Fleishauer is a "bad hair day" Yorkie mix with a sweet and silly personality. She spends a lot of her energy protecting her home and family and then rests on her loved ones' laps. She is small in stature but has a huge heart, and is always quick to make us smile.

Gracie Young was Kris's beloved corgi-shepherd mix. She helped inspire our pet lovers' devotional series. Though she doesn't have a story in this book, we celebrate her great heart and spirit and honor her memory.

Part I

Tales to Tug Your Heart

🐾 Champagne 🐾

The Dog Who Wouldn't Fight

Choose Love

Choices are the hinges of destiny.
PYTHAGORAS

When my friend Sue came home from work one summer evening in 2002, the last thing she dreamed of finding on her doorstep was a puppy. She loved dogs and had two of her own, but she was cautious. She could tell this pup was a pit bull, and the dog was emaciated. But as she carefully drew nearer, the four-footed stranger smiled and wagged its tail. When Sue sat beside the pup, it climbed on her lap, smothered her with kisses, and wrapped its paws lovingly around her neck.

Since Sue could not remember seeing this pup in the neighborhood, she decided to keep it overnight and check for lost dog flyers in the morning. She felt it prudent not to put the newcomer in the house with her own dogs. After feeding and watering the hungry foundling, Sue made a bed of blankets on her garage floor. The pup immediately curled up and went to sleep.

Later that evening a teenage boy knocked on Sue's door. He was looking for a missing pooch. Since his description fit the puppy perfectly, Sue returned the dog and thought that would be the end of the story.

It was just the beginning! Next evening, the female pit bull puppy was back. The poor thing looked literally "hang-dog," as if she'd done something wrong and expected to be beaten. Once again, the young pit bull showered Sue with kisses. Sensing the dog was in trouble, Sue called local animal control for advice. After confirming Sue's address, they told her there had been reports of people in a nearby house raising pit bulls to fight. The next day arrests were made in the case, and Sue was allowed to keep the loving puppy she named Champagne. "Champ" made instant friends with Sue's other dogs and has grown into a gentle giant who cuddles under the covers at night and is one of the sweetest canines Sue has ever met.

How Champ knew to flee that fighting environment is a mystery. Why she sought refuge on Sue's porch is as well. But one thing is clear: this pit bull puppy chose love—just as Sue did by taking her in. Those choices blessed them with each other and changed both their lives forever.

My friends Ruett and Rhonda also chose love. They did so in the face of wrenching tragedy. One night when their sons were small, Rhonda and the boys were at a local park where seven-year-old Evan played in sports leagues. Rhonda was about to drive off with Evan and ten-month-old Alec when gunfire erupted around their car. They were caught in the middle of gang violence. Both boys were hit. Alec suffered loss of vision from metal fragments that penetrated his eye. Evan was fatally shot. Rhonda got in the back with Evan until the paramedics beckoned her to come with them.

There are no words I could ever write that would adequately describe the excruciating pain Evan's parents suffered...and still suffer. It is searing to lose a child under any circumstances. This was a sudden, traumatic, utterly senseless loss. Nevertheless, in the midst of their pain Rhonda and Ruett made an amazing choice.

They knew Jesus as their personal Savior and Lord. They knew that unthinkable as it might be in their human strength, God was calling them to forgiveness and reconciliation. They chose love over hate, forgave those involved in their son's death, and formed the nonprofit Evan Leigh Foster Foundation. Its mission is to reach out to gang members with the message of God's love and redemption. They have shared that message personally, one on one. They hope and pray that by bringing gang members to faith in the God who can heal and transform them, gang violence will lessen and other children's lives will be spared. Their choice to love has changed their own and others' lives eternally and made them a living illustration of Romans 8:28: "And we know that in all things God works for the good of those who love him, who have been called according to his purpose."

A first-century martyr named Stephen would have understood their choice. He also chose to love those who caused him pain. He was seized and accused of blasphemy because he proclaimed that Jesus was the Messiah and the Son of God. Stephen chose to affirm his faith and defend it biblically. His accusers responded by stoning him. As he was on the brink of death, he prayed for his executioners. Acts 7:60 tells us that he "fell on his knees and cried out, 'Lord, do not hold this sin against them.' When he had said this, he fell asleep."

Champ the dog chose to flee fight training and live out her life loving both dogs and people. Rhonda and Ruett chose to reach out in love and forgive. Stephen chose to pray for those who were martyring him, even as their stones were crushing him to death. Though they all suffered, they did not let pain twist and embitter them. They chose love, and became a blessing to others. Their choices mattered, and so do ours. If we love and obey the Lord and let His love and forgiveness flow through us, even in our toughest times, who knows what difference we might make?

But God demonstrates his own love for us in this: While we were still sinners, Christ died for us (Romans 5:8).

Consider This:

Have you ever chosen to love in difficult circumstances? How did it affect you and others? Are you struggling with such a choice right now? If so, is there someone you might ask to support you in prayer?

The Gift of Life
Love Makes Sacrifices

The only gift is a portion of thyself.
RALPH WALDO EMERSON

Baby was a beautiful little boxer who lived with two larger dogs in Rodger and Margy's backyard. Their house was vacant for the moment. Rodger and Margy were getting settled in a new city, and had left their dogs and kids behind temporarily. The children, Quentin and Dylan, were staying with grandparents who lived near their old house. The boys went back home every day to feed the dogs and play with them.

One day the bigger dogs got out of hand and treated Baby badly. When Quentin came to check on the dogs he found that Baby had been seriously injured and needed medical attention. He called his grandma, Darlene, who hurried to his side. Darlene fought back the tears as they gently wrapped Baby in a blanket and rushed her to the veterinarian's office.

Baby's compassionate vet examined her with knowledge and empathy. She needed lots of stitches and staples to put her back together. But unlike the famous nursery rhyme character Humpty Dumpty, there was more involved than repairing Baby's outer "shell." She had lost a great deal of blood—so much that the vet was concerned she might not make it through the night.

Rather than leaving her with the night staff and going home to a well-deserved rest, Baby's vet went and fetched his own beloved yellow Lab, Jake. He extracted Jake's blood and shared it with Baby. Without the extra platelets from Jake, Baby might have died. The assisting vet also stayed after hours with Baby and lovingly kept her covered with warm blankets, meeting her every need. This was necessary because Baby was in shock.

Baby's human family was also in shock. They all loved Baby. Why, they wondered, would the other dogs treat her this way? The night was a long one for everybody. They prayed for Baby's healing and that she would be relieved from all pain.

The next morning, Baby's humans were anxious to see how she was doing, praying she was still alive. When they arrived at the vet's office, they found a happy puppy standing by the door of her cage waiting for them. She was well on her way to recovery. The whole family was deeply grateful to the vet for his sacrificial gifts of love, time, and Jake's platelets. Baby now lives a quiet life with one other—much calmer—little boxer.

Jake's gift of blood gave Baby another chance at life. My gift of blood gave someone another chance too. I had never given blood before, but the son of my husband's acquaintance was in a life-threatening circumstance. He needed surgery to live. His blood type was rare so they were asking anyone they knew to give blood if it matched his. Mine did, so I decided this was the time to share it. I went down to the blood bank and gave my blood for this young fellow. I never met him, but the surgery was a success and he recovered well. I'd always thought that giving blood was a huge sacrifice, but I realized it was a small sacrifice and a huge honor. I was glad to do it.

Jake and I gave blood rather painlessly and in sterile surroundings.

We didn't have to die to share it, either. That was not the case with God's Son. Jesus was horribly and hatefully beaten, then hung on a cross to shed His blood and die for our sins so we could have eternal life. Thankfully, He didn't stay dead. After three days He rose, just as He'd promised. He met with some of His followers and then went to heaven to prepare a place for all those who accept Him as their Savior.

Jake's master gave his dog's blood to save one boxer pup. I gave my blood to help save one man. Jesus gave His blood to save the world. If, like Baby, we receive the life-giving gift we've been offered, we will live in God's presence forever!

Then he took a cup, and when he had given thanks, he gave it to them, saying, "Drink from it, all of you. This is my blood of the covenant, which is poured out for many for the forgiveness of sins" (Matthew 26:27-28).

Consider This:

Have you ever given blood? What was it like for you? How did you feel about it? When did you last thank Jesus for giving His blood for you? Is there someone you'd like to tell about Jesus's sacrifice so that they might have a chance at eternal life?

Freeing Shadow
Perfect Love Casts Out Fear

Love is the magician that pulls
man out of his own hat.
BEN HECHT

Jennifer and her husband, Lynn, already had Panda, a two-year-old Tibetan terrier whom they had adopted from a stable, loving home. This dog was an "easy child"—affectionate, outgoing, and healthy right from the start.

Shadow was a different story. A six-year-old terrier/toy poodle mix, he was abandoned by his original owners and wandered the streets in the East San Fernando Valley until the pound picked him up. He was adopted soon after, but a year later the family returned him because their house was in foreclosure. On top of that, he had developed a leg injury. He was now "damaged goods," which minimized his chances of adoption.

Jennifer, however, fell in love with Shadow the minute she saw his picture on the rescue website. Shadow had the same coloring and markings as Panda—jet-black coat with a white chest and front paws, and melting brown eyes. So she and Lynn arranged to have Shadow meet Panda to see how they got along. They didn't kill each other, so Jennifer and Lynn signed the adoption papers and became a family of four.

They quickly found out their new kid was *not* Panda. Instead of being a people-pup, he was standoffish and skittish. When Lynn came near, Shadow would growl and hiss. Jennifer had to do a lot of coaxing to get Shadow to come, whereas Panda was always craving attention.

Shadow's leg problem compounded his negativity. He was often lethargic and cranky. If Jennifer and Lynn pushed too hard to engage him, Shadow hobbled off and hid, not wanting to be bothered, sometimes foregoing food. He would squeeze into the narrowest and most insular spots in the house. His favorite hiding place was underneath Lynn and Jennifer's heavy and immovable bed, so flushing him out was often an exercise in frustration. He refused to be sweet-talked, biting and snarling more viciously than his owners could believe. Jennifer would finally put on a protective mitt to reach under the bed and grab at him—but then the little stinker would dart to the other side. They kept their bedroom door closed to cut down on those episodes.

It took lots of loving, gentle coaxing, and great endurance for bites and snarls, but after about six months of being with his family, Shadow began to lower his defenses. The turning point came shortly after a new medication began to ease his leg pain. Instead of indifference when Panda walked by, Shadow crouched down, wagged his tail, and pounced on his unsuspecting housemate. Jennifer's heart was touched. From that moment on, the pups began to pal around and even snuggle up together in bed. They would never have done that in the early days.

Soon, Shadow was spending time in the living room instead of retreating to his hiding places, and would even cry out when he wanted to be picked up or held. As his leg improved, he became bouncy and animated, even approaching other people with a wagging tail! When Jennifer's sister visited for Thanksgiving, Shadow followed her everywhere, and loved cuddling up to her on the couch.

Jennifer and Lynn soon discovered Shadow *loved* belly rubs! A few well-placed scratches would send him rolling over, mouth opened wide with ecstasy. He even took to licking his people's hands or faces and recently graduated to giving lavish Eskimo kisses! That's quite a milestone for a former canine "affection Scrooge."

When Jennifer first told me about Shadow, I wondered why they'd kept that scared, snapping, snarling, hissing misanthrope so long. Why didn't they give him back? They had no idea he'd eventually come around to being the sweet and lovable dog he is today. Why bring home a gimpy middle-aged hostile street urchin when they could have just as easily adopted a sweet, adorable pick-of-the-litter purebred puppy?

Because…

When Jennifer said she fell in love with him at first sight, she did *not* mean it in a lightweight, teen romance novel, pop-song "groovy kind of love" way. Jennifer's love for Shadow was the same kind of love parents have for their kids and God has for us. It's that 1 Corinthians 13 kind of love: patient, kind, protective, trusting, hoping, and persevering. This Super Love, when applied in generous amounts over time to those who have been wounded by abandonment and abuse, has the most incredible healing effect.

First John 4:18 says, "There is no fear in love. But perfect love drives out fear." Jennifer and Lynn brought Shadow into a loving home and over time, the root fear of abandonment and abuse was driven out. What was left behind was the treasure of a real family.

We humans who suffer from similar issues of abandonment and abuse, who hide in narrow places and snap, snarl, and bite when others try to reach out to us, are also offered a healing kind of love. It's God's love, and it's meant to bring us into relationship with our true family. God paid a much higher price for this love than Jennifer and Lynn did in working with Shadow. But this love is the source of the ultimate transformation of the heart—and just like it did with Shadow, this love will set us free.

Jesus cast seven demons out of a woman named Mary Magdalene. His love transformed her into one of His most devoted followers. Then Jesus called a tax collector named Matthew to follow Him. Matthew responded to that love-inspired invitation, turned from his old life, and went on to write a book of the Bible.

Love has the power to transform demon-possessed women, unscrupulous tax collectors, and antisocial dogs.

Love has the power to transform the world.

Love has the power to transform you and me.

Beloved, let us love one another, for love is from God; and everyone who loves is born of God and knows God.... for God is love (1 John 4:7-8 NASB).

Consider This:

How has fear held you back in your life? How has love transformed and freed you? Who might God be calling you to reach out to with His love?

The Saga of Walter Brennan
Love Doesn't Count the Cost

For it is in giving that we receive.
ST. FRANCIS OF ASSISI

I had the immense privilege of spending a week with Walter Brennan toward the end of his life. Not Walter Brennan the actor—Walter Brennan the dog. He was in rough shape when my cousin Elly and her husband, Jim, took him in, but he blessed and changed their lives forever.

Walter was a big red Hungarian vizsla. He was pre-owned, but his family had gone through a rough patch. That's how he wound up with a rescue group at the age of seven. At this point his name was Damon. Elly spied him on a website. He was oversized for a vizsla and a bit goofy-looking, but Elly found this endearing—and called his rescue group.

Elly and Jim already had two vizslas, Willie and Bonnie. She was looking for a pal for them. What she learned about Damon sounded promising. He had a couch potato side that would suit Willie well. But he also loved to run, which would make him a fun friend for Bonnie. Was this a match made in doggie heaven?

Maybe—but there were medical issues. Damon had hurt his knee, undergone surgery, and was fighting infection. He was currently running on three legs. Elly's vet reviewed Damon's case and believed she knew what was causing the trouble. She thought she could probably fix him with a new surgery. But Damon also had heartworm disease. This can be transmitted by mosquitoes—which abound where Elly lives. She was concerned for her other dogs and felt she couldn't take Damon until he was heartworm-free. It took six months, but he was finally cleared for adoption.

Damon still had an infected leg and was fifteen pounds underweight. Elly and Jim knew his medical bills might mount, but they wanted to help this dog. Elly went and got him. He was home!

Damon fit in right from the start. He loved everyone, but especially Elly's young grandson, Jake. The first time Damon saw Jake, he let out a "cry of joy." They bonded instantly. Not until later did Elly learn that Damon had been trained as a special needs dog for his first family's little boy.

Elly and Jim didn't think the name Damon fit their oversized, underweight, gimpy new family addition. But what should they call him instead? The answer came in the form of a movie. After they'd had the dog a week, they were watching a Walter Brennan film. In the movie, Walter's character was tall, lean, and had a limp. Since Jim and Elly's last name is Brennan, the answer was obvious. They would call their new family member Walter.

Fixing their new dog's name was easy; fixing his body, not so much. The infection in Walter's leg moved to his eye. Their vet fought to save the eye with medication, but feared he might lose it. This was about the time I came to visit.

I remember Walter being sweet, loving, and uncomplaining despite his health problems. We took Walter on short walks to exercise his gimpy leg without straining him too much. His eye infection responded to medication, and the vet thought he could see shadows. He would never get his full vision back, but at least the eye would not have to come out.

The bad news was that the bills were mounting, despite price breaks from their sympathetic vet. Elly and Jim didn't flinch. They were committed. Walter had knee surgery and seemed to be recovering well, but then he developed pneumonia. His poor body had been through too much. He fought for two weeks but couldn't shake the illness. It seemed he would have to be put down.

Elly took Walter to her vet. There was a chapel area of the clinic where such things were done. Even as she and Walter sat waiting, she struggled with her decision. Suddenly, Walter stood up and headed for the door. She followed to retrieve him. He turned, looked at her, and collapsed in her arms. Walter was gone. Elly believes his last gift was sparing her that agonizing choice.

In the three months he spent with them, Walter gave Elly and her family many other gifts as well. He was full of love and had patience with everyone. He was very attuned to people and seemed to sense what each one needed. Elly thinks this was because of his special needs training. Walter was also a joyful dog, in spite of his medical problems. He taught his humans what it meant to make the most of each day. He touched many people's lives—and that didn't stop with his death.

Maybe Walter had gone away, but his medical bills hadn't budged. Elly and Jim were retired, but they had a plan. They applied for jobs as Santa and Mrs. Claus at a nearby Busch Gardens and got hired.

"Mrs. Claus" was expected to pass out cookies in the seasonal Christmas shows. But Walter had died the Tuesday before Thanksgiving, and the first show was just three days later. Elly was grieving, and she wasn't sure she could manage this. Sympathetic coworkers got her through. Walter inspired them to uplift her, and she followed his precious example of perseverance in adversity. Jim and

Elly brought a smile to many a child's face, and, in the process, joy-fully paid down their dog's debt.

Elly and Jim gave sacrificially of themselves for the love of a dog. Jesus gave infinitely more for us. He died an agonizing death to pay the sin debt for every person who ever has or ever will live. Contemplating His sacrifice made Jesus sweat blood in the garden of Gethsemane. But He went through with it anyway. Why? Because He loves us with an incomprehensible love! That's why the apostle Paul wrote to the Ephesians, "And I pray that you, being rooted and established in love, may have power, together with all the Lord's holy people, to grasp how wide and long and high and deep is the love of Christ, and to know this love that surpasses knowledge—that you may be filled to the measure of all the full-ness of God" (Ephesians 3:17-19).

Love gives sacrificially. It doesn't count the cost. It doesn't even look at the price tag. It delights to give and bless. God loves and gives to us this way, and if we do this for others, we will be like Him and share in His joy!

Now I (Paul) am ready to visit you for the third time, and I will not be a burden to you, because what I want is not your possessions but you...So I will very gladly spend for you everything I have and expend myself as well (2 Corinthians 12:14-15).

Consider This:

Has someone ever loved you sacrificially? What did this involve? What effect did it have on you? Is God calling you to love someone else in this way?

Squitchey Love
Being There Says You Care

No road is long with good company.
TURKISH PROVERB

Our daughter Karen works at Disneyland. Last time we were there, I watched a little girl dressed in a princess gown jumping up and down, waving her wand as if to create magic. Her excitement— and the happy giggles and dancing feet of other eager guests— reminded me of how excited our dog Squitchey gets when Karen comes home to see us.

Squitchey knows before any of us when Karen is arriving. She seems to recognize the particular sound of Karen's car. When Karen drives up, Squitchey bounds in the doggie door and races through the house to our back entrance. She whines and jumps until Karen comes in. Karen has no choice but to greet her first. Then our other dog, Stuart, gets his hug. Afterwards they all go outside to play ball. Finally Squitchey settles down on Karen's lap or by her side as we all listen to her adventures.

When Karen came home to Bakersfield for Christmas last year, she got a serious sinus infection. She felt miserable and had to stay with us an extra week. Squitchey rarely left her side. When Karen slept on the couch or sat in the easy chair, Squitchey perched on her lap or curled up next to her. When Karen went to the bathroom, Squitchey followed and waited impatiently by the door.

After Karen's fever was gone and she was feeling better, she started to pack to return to Anaheim. Squitchey followed her around the house. When Karen stopped in one place, Squitchey would lie down flat with her ears drooping, realizing her dear human friend would be leaving soon. Finally it was time for Karen to go. She hugged Squitchey good-bye. Squitchey dragged herself slowly out to the backyard and slept most of the afternoon.

Watching Squitchey's devotion and commitment to Karen reminds me of my husband's love for me. Steve and I have been married over 38 years and I can't imagine us not being by each other's side. Last Sunday I got sick during church and Steve took me home and stayed with me rather than going to the second service to play his trombone in the praise band. He felt that his place was with me. I am sure that his loving care helped me to heal quickly. That's the way we have been with each other since we were teenagers—except our commitment has grown deeper over the years.

Steve is a farmer. One day after a big rain, I wanted to go with him to some rain-soaked fields thick with mud. I was no help— I was just along for the ride and the company. It was good that he had four-wheel drive or we would still be out there! We went mud bogging, sliding all over the road. When we reached our destination, Steve's pickup truck was covered in mud. It could have been tense, but we had a great time because we were together.

Squitchey is devoted to Karen. Steve is devoted to me. The Old Testament prophet Elisha was devoted to his mentor, Elijah. God had commanded Elijah to anoint Elisha as his successor. Elisha became Elijah's attendant, and he stayed close to Elijah for years. Finally, the day came for God to take Elijah to be with Him. Three times as they were traveling, Elijah told Elisha to remain behind.

Three times, Elisha refused. He stayed right beside his spiritual father until Elijah "went up to heaven in a whirlwind" (2 Kings 2:11). Like Squitchey, Elisha was grieved to see his master go—and tore his clothes as a sign of that grief. Then he picked up Elijah's prophetic mantle and faithfully served God all the rest of his days.

Squitchey stayed with Karen. Steve and I stayed with each other. Elisha stayed with Elijah. For each of us, it was a commitment of love. It's the same love God shows His children when He promises never to leave or forsake us. I am so grateful that I have a God and a husband and a dog that will be there and care—because they want to be!

Love never fails (1 Corinthians 13:8).

Consider This:

Who in your life has stayed close by you through the good times and the down times? What has this meant to you? Who might God want you to do this for? What are some ways you have felt God being there and caring for you?

Jazzmin's "Ian Watch"
Who Do You Long For?

Sometimes, when one person is missing,
the whole world seems depopulated.

ALPHONSE DE LAMARTINE

My friend Val and her family absolutely adore Jazzmin, their 13-year-old Airedale terrier. She adores them too…especially Ian. Val's middle son lived at home long after his brothers flew the coop. He became Jazzmin's special person. Jazzmin waited eagerly for Ian to get home from work every day. She hung out with him all evening and sacked out in his room when he went to bed. True, she'd be curled up on the living room sofa by morning, but she always started out snoozing with her best buddy.

That was all before Ian's life changed. He decided to move from Los Angeles to California's central coast. He had a great job opportunity and had always thought about living in this area. He felt the change would be good and found a wonderful place to live. Though sad to see him go, his parents were excited about the new vistas opening in his life. They were glad for him.

Jazzmin was bummed!

Her doggie brain didn't understand what was happening. She

just knew her pal Ian was no longer there. She seemed depressed. She would hang out by the front door, then stretch out in Ian's old room to sleep, just like she had before he left. Was she waiting, hoping he would someday come home to her?

Maybe so. And one day he did, if just for a little while. He had returned to get his bed and haul it to his new home.

When Ian walked through the front door, Jazzmin went berserk. She is a senior dog, but she kicked up her heels like a six-month-old puppy! She literally jumped for joy. She rose up on her hind legs, wrapped her paws around Ian's thighs, and gave him a doggie hug. She was a living doggie portrait of pure delight. It blew Ian away. He hadn't realized he was quite that important to Jazzmin, and his heart was warmed by the love of his canine friend.

Jazzmin's sweet, innocent attachment to Ian reminds me of how small children often long for their parents when they are apart. When I was very young, I went through a period when I hated being left with babysitters. I think I was somehow afraid that my parents wouldn't come back, or that something might happen to them. I remained wakeful, waiting to close my eyes until they were safely home.

I also recall one specific incident when Mom went to the grocery store. For some reason I was petrified she wouldn't return. More than half a century later, I can't recall if she'd gotten upset with me or if there was some other trigger. I do have a sense that I stood at the window, looking out at the street, hoping for a glimpse of her and bawling my eyes out.

Like most children, I outgrew such separation anxiety as I got older. After my dad died when I was 30, I'm ashamed to say I saw a lot less of my mom than she would have wanted. Fortunately, in the years right before her death some of that got fixed. But she let me know that my lack of longing to be in her presence hurt her, and I'd sent a message that I didn't really love her.

God also wants us to long for Him. He wants us to delight in being with Him, just as Jazzmin rejoiced in being with Ian. Just as Jazzmin looked forward to her special together time with Ian each day, God wants us to treasure our daily special time with Him. But He also sent His Son, Jesus, to die for our sins, rise from the dead, and ascend into heaven to intercede for us. And one day Jesus will return—not to collect His things, like Ian did, but to remain and reign over us forever. God wants us to watch and wait eagerly for that day too. And unlike Jazzmin, we can be certain of our Master's return. God promises us this in His Word. In Acts 1:10-11 we read that the disciples "were looking intently up into the sky as [Jesus] was going, when suddenly two men dressed in white stood before them. 'Men of Galilee,' they said, 'why do you stand here looking into the sky? This same Jesus, who has been taken from you into heaven, will come back in the same way you have seen him go into heaven.'"

Jesus doesn't want us to be depressed, as Jazzmin was, because He has clearly told us He will return. He wants us to wait expectantly by being alert to the signs of the times and by going about His business. In Matthew 24:45-47, He said, "Who then is the faithful and wise servant, whom the master has put in charge of the servants in his household to give them their food at the proper time? It will be good for that servant whose master finds him doing so when he returns. Truly I tell you, he will put him in charge of all his possessions."

Chances are Ian won't ever live with Jazzmin again. But he'll be back to visit, and she'll rejoice whenever she sees him. Jesus is with us now through His Spirit, and one day He will return for good to reign and rule on this earth. If we rejoice in this promise and wait eagerly for Him, it will warm His heart, just as Jazzmin warmed Ian's!

Therefore keep watch, because you do not know on what day your Lord will come (Matthew 24:42).

Consider This:

Are you eager to spend time with the Lord every day? How do you do this? What is special about your time together? Are you anticipating Jesus's second coming? How are you watching and waiting for Him?

Hopelessly Devoted to You
Love Is Faithful

He is your friend, your partner, your defender, your dog. You are his life, his love, his leader. He will be yours, faithful and true, to the last beat of his heart. You owe it to him to be worthy of such devotion.

ANONYMOUS

Erika was six when her family got Missy, a yellow Lab/golden retriever mix. The two girls bonded instantly—like best friends and sisters of a different species. Erika spent all her free time with Missy in those early childhood days that seemed to last forever. Her parents entrusted her with the responsibility of feeding Missy when she came home from school and taking Missy on her afternoon walks.

But as Erika grew older, she had more demands on her time. There was schoolwork, extracurricular activities, sports, hanging out with friends, church stuff—and it all added up to less time with Missy. Then, in high school, Erika had a shift in attitude. She started feeling like she was just too cool for her dog. It was like she was part of the in crowd and Missy was a four-legged nerd with a tail. Erika began to take Missy for granted.

Missy did not respond in kind. Her devotion to Erika never wavered. Through Erika's transition from kid to teen, Missy was constantly loyal and loving no matter how little time Erika spent with her. Missy held no grudges. She didn't complain. She was always there when Erika needed a friend. Sounds like Missy was exercising that 1 Corinthians 13 "love is patient, love is kind" brand of love.

Like many teens, Erika had some terrible angst-ridden days in high school when she didn't feel like sharing her problems with any of her family or friends. They wouldn't understand. They would half-listen in their busyness. They'd offer well-meaning but tired old clichés she didn't need. It was times like this that Erika would go out to the backyard and visit with Missy.

Good ol' Missy was always there. She wouldn't be on the phone, playing computer games, working on a project, or in the middle of an addictive TV series. Missy was a 24/7 friend. She had amazing intuition and knew exactly how to minister to Erika. Sometimes they'd play. Other times they'd just sit on the grass and stare into space together. Missy would know exactly when to turn to Erika and give her a little lick on the cheek. It was magic. Erika's gloom would lift and a smile would break through. The six-year-old in Erika would return and she'd blow on Missy's nose, triggering Missy's turbo lick response. Next thing you knew, Missy would be licking Erika's face like an ice cream cone. It would have looked gross to an outside observer but it was pure joy for Erika and Missy.

Erika didn't realize how important Missy was to her until she moved out to go to college. When Erika felt down, she couldn't just pop into the backyard and let Missy lick away her blues. She couldn't call Missy up and have a heart-to-heart. And since keypads aren't exactly paw-friendly, forget texting. So for those college years, Erika and Missy had to wait for a school break or summer to be together. They went for walks or sat outside staring into other dimensions, just enjoying being in each other's presence.

In between her junior and senior year, Erika decided to move to Los Angeles for the summer. She was a film major and wanted to explore the possibilities in the entertainment capital of the world. It was during this time that her parents called and told her Missy had cancer. Erika's immediate thought was to go home and be there for her dear friend of 15 years. Erika could barely remember a time when Missy wasn't in her life. They had literally grown up together.

But Erika had a job in LA. She had made new friends, and one in particular that made her stay amazingly memorable. She grew up in new ways and realized that her experiences over this summer were profoundly shaping her future. It was a very exciting time.

Then there was Missy, 2,000 miles away in the tiny Midwestern town of Hanover, Minnesota. Missy was in terrible pain and growing worse each day. Erika struggled, not knowing what to do. She couldn't drop everything right now and go back home—or could she? Feelings of guilt consumed her. She prayed God would keep Missy alive until summer was over, until she could finish what she came to LA to do.

Missy didn't make it. She died three weeks before Erika's planned return. The night her parents put Missy down, they tried to feed her but she wouldn't eat. She kept trying to stand but she'd just fall over with her tail wagging the whole time. Missy adored her family and to the very end tried to be the same cheerful, loving, and loyal dog she'd always been.

Erika still feels guilty she wasn't there when Missy needed her most. Was she just plain selfish for staying in LA the whole summer? If Erika had known in advance that Missy would get sick and pass away, maybe she would've put off the trip until later. Maybe she would've asked her parents to take Missy with her to California. Maybe this, maybe that.

There are no easy answers for Erika. There are no instant remedies or greeting card platitudes that will make everything better.

It's not like Erika can phone God's hotline to ask if she did the right thing. It'd be so nice if the Lord could FedEx a pill from heaven to instantly dissolve her feelings of guilt and selfishness—but that's not how it works.

We have all gone through times when we wonder if we did the right thing. Black-and-white guilt is easier in a way. But gray-area guilt is what we deal with more often.

Should I have come home earlier to spend time with my terminally ill dog?

Should I have worked less and spent more time with my children when they were young?

Should I have taken more time with my elderly parents before they died?

Once the time has passed, once the window of opportunity has closed, there is no second chance to do things over. There is only dealing with one's perception and memories.

If you are currently looking into a mirror and seeing a guilty face, whether it be in shades of gray or in stark black and white, there is a solution in Scripture. It doesn't promise to be a quick fix or easy answer. It just points you in the right direction to deal with your very real feelings of guilt and personal condemnation. It points you to a choice: to embrace or to reject a personal relationship with Christ. Unlike many other options in life, this window of opportunity, this invitation from Jesus, is available for as long as you live— no matter how guilty you feel, no matter what you've done.

With the arrival of Jesus, the Messiah, that fateful dilemma is resolved. Those who enter into Christ's being-here-for-us no longer have to live under a continuous, low-lying black cloud. A new power is in

operation. The Spirit of life in Christ, like a strong wind, has magnificently cleared the air, freeing you from a fated lifetime of brutal tyranny at the hands of sin and death (Romans 8:1-2 MSG).

Consider This:

Who are your most hopelessly devoted friends and loved ones? How have they been faithful to you? How have you been there for them? How has God shown Himself faithful in your life?

A Crate and a Manger
When We Fail, God's Love Doesn't

Though our feelings come and go,
God's love for us does not.
C.S. LEWIS

Morgan was a little Sheltie mix I adopted as a two-year-old rescue. He saw me as his savior and adored me. I adored him too—but not his bathroom habits. He kept having accidents in the house. I was told it would help the training process if I crated him when I couldn't keep an eye on him.

Christmas afternoon was one of those times. I was going visiting for several hours, and hoping to prevent any mishaps, I left Morgan in his crate. When I got home that night, it seemed the tactic had succeeded. I let him and my other dog, Biscuit, out to do their business. Once they were back inside, I went to change clothes. In that short time, Morgan messed in the house yet again. In spite of all my efforts, he'd still blown it. And I lost it.

I knew I loved this dog dearly. I knew my yard was fenced and gated. I knew I didn't mean what was coming out of my mouth. But I needed to vent. I put Morgan outside, in the fenced and gated yard, and told him to go live somewhere else.

Three minutes later I was running up the outdoor steps to my back fence, calling the little guy. When he came I gathered him in my arms. I plopped down on a step, wept into his fur, and told him that no matter what he did, I would always love him. I told him he was going nowhere. He was mine, no matter how badly he blew it, no matter how many times he messed.

Suddenly, out in the cold on Christmas night, with my little dog in my arms, it hit me. What a picture of my relationship with God! Through faith in Jesus's death for my sins, I was adopted into God's family...just as I'd adopted Morgan into mine. But I still sinned. I still kept "messing." Even so, God didn't put me out and tell me to go live somewhere else. He loved me so much that He was not willing to part with me, even though I deserved it (so much more than my dog did). So, figuratively speaking, He did with me what I did with Morgan. He gathered me into His lap, wept over me, and forgave me.

God used that Christmas experience with Morgan as a living parable in my life to pull back a curtain on the depths of His love. Centuries earlier, He did the same with the prophet Hosea. God asked Hosea to make his life a living illustration to Israel, showing them that despite their messes, His love would stay true. He told Hosea to marry an adulteress. Hosea took Gomer to be his wife, but she was unfaithful—just as Israel had been unfaithful to God. God told Hosea to go after Gomer and redeem her. In Hosea 3:1-2 we read, "The LORD said to me, 'Go, show your love to your wife again, though she is loved by another man and is an adulteress. Love her as the LORD loves the Israelites, though they turn to other gods and love the sacred raisin cakes.' So I bought her for fifteen shekels of silver and about a homer and a lethek of barley."

Ultimately, God bought all of us with the precious blood of His Son.

Morgan's accidents lessened in time, but he never had a perfect record. Neither have I, in this life! But what the training crate of the law couldn't do, a manger could. God sent His Son to clean up my sin mess so that despite my failures, I can bask in His unfailing love forever!

*Israel, put your hope in the L*ORD*, for with the L*ORD *is unfailing love and with him is full redemption. He himself will redeem Israel from all their sins (Psalm 130:7-8).*

Consider This:

Can you think of a time when you "messed," but the people it hurt loved you anyway? How did this impact your life? How has God loved you even when you let Him down? Is there someone in your life God is calling you to love this way?

Diablo, Or Not?
Love Can Conquer Our Devils

Darkness cannot drive out darkness; only
light can do that. Hate cannot drive
out hate; only love can do that.
MARTIN LUTHER KING, JR.

The pressing question for Ryan on one never-to-be-forgotten night was whether the name would fit. That applied both to the girl he was taking on their first date, and the big, growling dog he would have to get past to do it.

Actually, Ryan had only the highest expectations for the girl. He loved her name—Bella, which means beautiful. He thought she was the most gorgeous girl he had ever met in his young life. They'd gotten to know each other at school. They were in a few classes together and talked at lunch. Her smile lit up her face and brightened Ryan's world every time he saw it. He loved telling her silly stories about his fishing and hunting trips and seeing her grin in response.

Bella gave Ryan the impression that she liked him, so asking her out seemed like a natural next step. When she said she'd love to go, he wanted to jump up and down and shout for joy. But he kept his cool. He suggested going to a restaurant and movie—both of her choice. She happily agreed, and the date was set.

On the big night, Ryan was a bundle of excitement and nerves. Bella had told him where she lived and how to get there. Her home was on the other side of town from his, in a poorer community. The house was on a corner lot. The street was filled with children playing a wild game of kickball.

Ryan parked his car on a side street, away from the children, and walked up the steps to the wraparound front porch. He stopped to straighten his clothes and brush his hair. He had not yet met her parents and desperately wanted to make a good impression. Right about then, a growling pit bull rounded the corner of the house and started after him. He had no time to think. He dashed in the front door and slammed it shut behind him.

Ryan stood with his back to the wall, breathing heavily. He'd been too panicked to consider that he had just barged into some-one's home unannounced. He saw three people heading toward him to confront him. First was a man who appeared to be Bella's father. Right behind was an older fellow—likely Bella's granddad. Bringing up the rear was a young boy. Ryan figured him to be the little brother she had talked so much about. But where was Bella?

Ryan tried to introduce himself. The two men regarded him with a confused and somewhat angry stare. The little boy said his name was Raul and asked why Ryan was in their home. Ryan explained that he'd come to pick up Bella for a date. Raul translated these words for his still rather hostile-looking elders.

At last, the two men broke into huge smiles. Then they started howling with laughter, and Raul joined in. They shook Ryan's hand and Raul revealed that his sister hadn't told any of them about her date. She had gone next door to borrow a cup of sugar for her mom and would return shortly.

Once everyone had settled down, Ryan asked about the huge

pit bull who had growled at him. He explained that the dog was the reason for his rapid, unexpected entrance into their home. Was the dog rabid or just a crazy wild animal?

After Raul translated this, all three of them guffawed again—even more loudly than before. Raul explained that the dog, Diablo, was their pet. He was really a very sweet dog, but he was protective of his family. They had rescued him from the desert when he was just a puppy. He'd been left there to fend for himself. Passersby had thrown things at him. He'd probably had to fight for food and become aggressive as a way of survival. When Bella's family found him he was hungry and tired and had a cut on his forehead.

They had caught the needy stray and brought him to their home. They'd taken care of him, fed him well, and loved him. At first he'd had a hard time responding positively. His nasty growl made them think of Satan, so they named him Diablo. They refused to give up on their devil dog. After a few weeks, he seemed to realize that love was better than hate. He accepted his new family and neighborhood. Since he was a devil no longer they considered changing his name, but he already knew it, so they left it.

Ryan feared Diablo's name still fit him rather well. When Bella's family let him in, Ryan stood frozen as Diablo slowly circled. Then Ryan warily stuck out his hand. To his great relief, Diablo licked it, and everyone laughed once more. Bella returned and apologized for not being there when Ryan arrived. The two went off for a wonderful evening—Ryan armed with a brand new story to tell her over dinner.

Human love healed Diablo's past hurts so he was a devil dog no longer. How much more can God's love heal and free us! Jesus's life and ministry are powerful proof of this. In some cases, He cast out literal demons, as with the Gerasene man who had multiple evil spirits (Mark 5:1-13). In other cases, His love healed and freed people from the "devils" of sin, guilt, shame, rejection, and hurt.

Diablo didn't stop being a devil dog the moment he was loved and cared for. It took time. But Bella's family stuck with him, and in the end, love conquered. Are there Diablos in your life who God is calling you to stick with and love until their devils are conquered too?

And now these three remain: faith, hope and love. But the greatest of these is love (1 Corinthians 13:13).

Consider This:

In what areas of your life have you been a growler, like Diablo? What underlying pain may have triggered this? How has God's love helped to free and transform you? How could your experience encourage someone else?

A Different Kind of Leash
God's Love Shows Restraint

Conscience whispers, but interest screams aloud.
JEAN ANTOINE PETIT-SENN

Daisy had been praying for a dog—not just any dog, but a dog God had picked out for her. So when a friend called to say her son had rescued an abused stray from a tough inner-city neighborhood, Daisy was intrigued. Then she saw the dog. She was greasy, flea-infested, covered with sores, had a cut nose, and her hair was falling out. A bath and a prayer later, Daisy decided to keep this scrappy street survivor—and named her Harriet.

Daisy soon took Harriet to meet her friend's dogs. On more than one occasion, Harriet muscled in and scavenged any food left in her host dogs' bowls. When the other dogs rightfully tried to reclaim their food, Harriet turned "wolf" and backed them off with snarls and bared fangs. Daisy commanded Harriet to stop, but Harriet couldn't restrain herself. She continued to gulp down the food, like she did on the streets, all the while keeping an aggressive eye on her more mannered peers. Daisy began to keep Harriet tightly leashed in the presence of other dogs. Harriet was off the street, but the street was still in Harriet.

Within the month, Harriet gave Daisy another surprise. This dog was pregnant, and in due time gave birth to a litter of five. Daisy was amazed to see this street dog with attitude suddenly turn mother, patiently allowing her hungry pups to suckle to their hearts' delight. When the little ones were old enough to be weaned off milk, Daisy spread out five bowls filled with puppy chow. She made sure each pup had its own spot, then proudly watched as they ate their first solid meal. But what caught Daisy's attention was Harriet's unusual behavior. She was sitting calmly to the side, watching her puppies gobble down their food. Normally, the sight of another dog dining would transform Harriet into a food-stealing bully. But Harriet restrained herself, *leashed* herself, and waited until her puppies finished their meal. Then and only then did she get up to eat from her own bowl. Daisy was impressed. Because of the special bond between mother and child, Harriet was able to restrain her selfish nature and put the needs and welfare of her pups ahead of her own. Daisy wound up keeping one of the puppies, a female named Cinco. To this day, Harriet restrains her old nature and allows her daughter Cinco to eat in peace.

Human parents are also called upon to exercise self-control. When it comes to playing games or sports with a young child, any mom or dad will tell you it often becomes an exercise in restraint.

When our son Skye was five, we put up a mini-basketball backboard in the house. It was mounted on the door, about six feet off the floor. This was almost double Skye's height and it was very challenging for him to make a basket—especially when he was playing against me. I could slam dunk at will and block any shot he could throw up. If I'd gone all out against my young son, I could easily have demolished him—and his spirit—scoring thousands to his zero. But because he was my son, because of our father-son bond, I restrained myself—something I would not have done if playing against someone my own size. With Skye, I missed shots. I slipped and fell so he could run circles around me. I pretended to block. I allowed him to double-dribble, to foul me, even tackle me and pull me down, all without penalty. Because I loved this little guy, I voluntarily leashed my powers and my competitive nature so he could have fun, enjoy the game, and feel good about winning.

A mother dog restrains her desire to eat first in deference to her pups. A human father restrains his superior athletic powers when playing basketball against his five-year-old son. If natural love has the power to inspire such restraint, what restraint might supernatural love inspire?

The Bible tells us. In the most amazing act of restraint in the history of the universe, the Son of God restrained His awesome divine power and went to the cross in obedience to His Father's will. He told His tormenters in Matthew 26:53, "Do you think I cannot call on my Father, and he will at once put at my disposal more than twelve legions of angels?"

God loved the world so much that He gave His only Son, who showed the ultimate restraint—so we could have the ultimate gift of eternal life.

He does not treat us as our sins deserve or repay us according to our iniquities. For as high as the heavens are above the earth, so great is his love for those who fear him (Psalm 103:10-11).

Consider This:

Have you ever felt God showing restraint toward you when

you didn't deserve it? How did it encourage you? How did it deepen your relationship with Him? Is God calling you to show loving restraint toward someone in your life right now? What would that look like?

Stuart's Heart Vision Goggles
It's What's Inside That Counts

*And now here is my secret, a very simple secret;
it is only with the heart that one can see rightly,
what is essential is invisible to the eye.*

ANTOINE DE SAINT-EXUPÉRY

I think I should hire Stuart to help me choose my friends. He seems to have a special instinct about people. It's as if he's got heart vision goggles that help him look past their outer appearance to their true inner selves.

Stuart is great at telling us which folks he does or doesn't like. If he's uncomfortable with whoever is coming into our home, he makes a big deal of barking and acting uneasy. If we allow them in anyway, he will keep barking at them or stick close to us and go into protective mode.

One time a salesman came to my door and wanted to sell me a cleaning product I had never heard of before. He showed me what it could do by using it to clean my front porch table. I was curious to find out more and he seemed safe enough, so I let him in. Stuart was very unhappy about this. He would not settle down. I tried to make him go outdoors, but he would have none of it. He stayed

53

right by my side the whole time the salesman was there. Every time
the man would get close to me in the course of showing his wares,
Stuart would growl at him. The man seemed harmless to me, but
later on in the day I noticed that the little calculator I had left on
the porch table was gone. Maybe Stuart knew more than I did.

Stuart is also quick to let us know when he likes someone. He
welcomes the visitor with bright eyes and happy woofs. This is what
he did the first time our daughter Christy brought a very special
young man named Steven home to meet us—a young man who
would become her husband.

Naturally, Steven was somewhat nervous to meet Christy's parents. Little did he know that he would first be vetted by our dog.
Stuart greeted Christy and then checked out her beau. Stuart's
calm, sweet spirit seemed to shout, "This guy can stay!" As Steven walked through the entry into our living room, Stuart barked
happily, inviting his new friend—well, actually *begging* him!—to
go outside and play ball. We all headed into the backyard and the
bonding began. Stuart stuck close to Steven for the rest of the evening, sitting beside him, smiling his goofy corgi smile.

To the world, Steven is a wonderful young man with a heart of
gold. Still, he's not royalty or a rock star. Steven has celebrity sta-
tus in Stuart's eyes, however. These days, Steven can't come into
our home without going straight to the backyard to join Stuart in
a game of ball. When they come back in, Stuart sits right beside
him. I've never seen him take to anyone as fast as he did Steven.
I'm sure he also may have sensed that Christy loved him, and that
helped his decision. But even so, his unconditional love surprised
us because it was so fast and easy. Our son, John, told Steven he had
never seen Stuart act like that. Even John himself had not gotten
Stuart's doggie stamp of approval as quickly as Steven did.

Stuart's sense of people is helpful, but he's still just a dog. God
can help us infinitely more. Our all-knowing Lord sees exactly

what's in people's hearts. Jesus demonstrated this during His earthly ministry. There were religious leaders in His day who looked fabulous on the outside, but Jesus called them "whitewashed tombs." He wasn't fooled by their outward charade of righteousness. He knew their hearts weren't right and they needed to confess their sin and come to Him for forgiveness. There were also people who, like Steven, were either quite normal-looking on the outside or looked downright "yucky" to the religious mucky-mucks. But Jesus knew their hearts were hungry for Him. He welcomed those folks, like Stuart welcomed Steven, and they became devoted followers of His. Some even made the "who's who" of famous biblical figures.

I prayed for Christy's husband all her life. When she brought Steven home, I felt confident that God had brought them together. Stuart didn't know this, but it was fun to get his confirmation. God is eager to give wisdom and discernment to all His children, if we will just ask. Will you let Him put His heart vision goggles on you?

Bring to an end the violence of the wicked and make the righteous secure—you, the righteous God who probes minds and hearts (Psalm 7:9).

Consider This:

Has a beloved pet's heart vision goggles ever saved you from trouble? What happened? How might you have been deceived, and why? What did you learn that might make you wiser next time? How has God's guidance regarding people saved you from missteps?

Anything but His Toes
God Cares About Our Fears

To suffering there is a limit; to fearing, none.
SIR FRANCIS BACON

Willie the dog has a phobia. It's not your normal doggie fear. He doesn't dread loud sounds or vet visits. He doesn't cringe when he's left home alone. No, this 60-pound Hungarian vizsla is overcome with terror by the sight of a human hand holding a dreaded *toenail clipper.*

He's been this way since my cousin Elly first adopted him at the age of 12 weeks. This was family number two for Willie. His first adoption was on September 11, 2001—really. To top it off, his breeder lived about five miles from the Pennsylvania site where one of the hijacked planes went down. It is tempting to think 9/11 might have played into Willie's oddball fear...but it isn't likely.

Willie wound up with Elly because his first family wanted to return him when they learned he had only one testicle. His breeder wouldn't take him back, and Willie landed in vizsla rescue. Elly and her husband, Jim, had recently lost both their own vizslas—one to old age, the other to illness. Someone called and told them about Willie. They grabbed him.

Willie's new humans noticed his toenail-clipping phobia right away. They speculate it was triggered by some puppyhood trauma. Elly recalls that his dewclaws weren't well clipped. But those were on his front feet, and his back feet are his major Achilles heel.

Elly told me Willie is extremely protective of his feet. He doesn't like them touched—especially his back ones. If she tries, he will tuck them under so she can't get to them. If you have a toenail clipper in your hand, his fear skyrockets. If he can, he launches through the doggie door and flees to the yard. If he's on a table to be groomed, he tries to throw himself off. He won't ever attempt to bite the hand that tries to clip his nails, but he'll do almost anything else to get away. Elly's main fear is that one day he'll hurt himself in his frantic struggles to escape.

Elly and Jim can't ask Willie why toenail-clipping makes him go berserk. But in the ten years they've had him, they've tried everything else. They've bought various kinds of clippers. They've tried an alternate nail-clipping tool. They've left clippers around the house so their dog would get used to seeing them. He could handle clippers on a stand, but not in a hand. He'd even go ballistic if those clippers were being used on his doggie sister, Bonnie.

Finally, Elly threw in the towel and decided to let her vet's techs trim Willie's toenails. Last time, it took two of them. One distracted Willie and fed him cookies while the other lifted one foot at a time and somehow managed the deed. *Not* clipping Willie's nails isn't an option because if they get too long, Willie might slip on Elly's hardwood floors. But she's already planning to have his nails done when his teeth are cleaned. He'll be put under anesthesia for the dental work, and he'll never know his toenails were part of the package.

Willie's persistent toenail-clipping phobia got me thinking about my own fears—specifically my fear of death. Like Willie, I've had this fear since I was very young. I can remember being about four years of age and dreading turning five, because I was a year closer to dying. Now that I've come to faith in Christ, I have the promise of eternal life to temper that fear—but I can't say it's gone. One of the ways it expresses itself these days is through another fear. I'm scared to be put completely out with anesthesia—because I might not wake up.

I'm at an age where my doctor would like me to get a colonoscopy. I've put it off partly due to this concern. When I had tooth implant surgery, I opted for a type of sedation that let me remain partially awake. When I faced arthroscopic knee surgery earlier this year, I wanted to do the same thing—but God had other plans.

I was told I could be awake for the surgery itself and watch. What I wasn't clear about until I was lying in the surgery center was that I would be knocked out initially. My anesthesiologist warned me I would not want to be awake when they gave me the shot to numb my knee. Hmm…virtually certain major pain versus phobia about highly unlikely death? I didn't insist.

Still, I was extremely scared. It didn't help when I heard the anesthesia they were using was the same drug that had gone so wrong with Michael Jackson. My anesthesiologist assured me it was excellent when used correctly. It would put me out instantly and I would awake as soon as it was stopped. My surgeon came in and got me laughing, and that helped. I'm not sure exactly when I went under. Next thing I knew, I was conscious and my surgeon was showing me the inside of my knee on a screen.

I'd been told if I felt pain during the procedure, I could say so and be put to sleep again. I doubted I'd want it that way. I was wrong. I started hurting. I said so—twice. When I "came to" again, the procedure was over. And my long-standing anesthesia phobia, though not gone, was greatly lessened.

Willie's a dog. Elly can't sit down and reason with him. She can't talk him down from his trauma, or even find out what it was. But

I'm a human. I have reasoning powers. And I have a loving God who has given me a whole host of His promises. Even so, I hung onto my fear. But instead of being angry or disgusted, God met me with understanding and love and gently worked me through it.

I wonder if Joshua had cold feet when he had to step into Moses's shoes and lead the Israelites into Canaan. We can't know—but we do know God kept reassuring him. In the first chapter of Joshua, God urges him to be strong and courageous three times in four verses. I don't think biblical courage means the absence of fear—I think it means being willing to obey God regardless. I believe God understands our fears and is waiting to graciously free us from them step by step if we will put our trust in Him.

Willie trusts Elly as much as he can, and her love covers the rest. God will lovingly work with us too, if we ask Him. No matter how great your fears may be, you can entrust them—and yourself—to a caring God who is bigger!

Even though I walk through the darkest valley, I will fear no evil, for you are with me; your rod and your staff, they comfort me (Psalm 23:4).

Consider This:

What are your greatest fears in life? Where did those fears come from? How have you tucked your toes or fled through the doggie door to escape what scares you? How might God be calling you to be strong and courageous instead? What Scriptures might encourage you in this?

The Dog That Stuck Closer Than a Brother

Love the Extra Mile

Friendship isn't a big thing—it's a million little things.
ANONYMOUS

My husband, Steve, and I both grew up near Bakersfield, California. After spending our first year of marriage elsewhere, we moved back. We lived in a little farmhouse next door to the home where Steve had grown up. This is where we adopted our first puppy.

McPherson was a beautiful shepherd mix we got from Steve's dad. He helped prepare me for the children we would have. He taught me how to be responsible for someone other than myself by feeding and caring for him. When Steve returned from a long day at work or I hauled a carload of groceries home, McPherson would be there to greet us. He didn't understand that we had to take care of ourselves. In his mind, we'd come home to play with him, so that's what we should do. There was no time to waste. Someone had to throw him a ball or roll with him in the grass.

From puppyhood, McPherson went to work with my farmer

husband, learning how to catch gophers. He also learned to protect, like a good dog should. McPherson would bark whenever a stranger entered our yard. If he felt unsure of a guest, he would stay watchfully by the door until the person left.

McPherson was protective of our children too. He watched them in his wonderful canine way, playing with them, loving all of us as we loved him.

He helped teach unconditional love by loving unconditionally himself. It never mattered how we looked or how we were feeling. He was always there to greet us and make us feel good to be home.

McPherson was just a puppy when my dad died. So was I. I was 21 years old then. When I was especially lonely for Dad, McPherson seemed to feel my pain. I remember sitting on the porch one day, watching a tractor plowing a field across the street. I'm sure McPherson would rather have been chasing after the tractor, but he stayed by my side and let me pet him, comforting me by his closeness and sweet spirit. As we sat, I remember seeing a kitty playing nearby. McPherson did too, but he remained with me. When I finally stood up, I hugged him and he seemed to hug me back. Then he gleefully ran after the kitty, not to hurt him but to play with him, for they were friends.

When we inadvertently ignored him, McPherson would either stay close beside us or gently walk away—but he never seemed angry. He was an incredibly loving dog. It was a comfortable evening to sit with him and tell him how I was feeling or share thoughts that no one else needed to know.

When McPherson was older, he didn't go out as much because of his arthritis. But he was sure glad when Steve got home so he could play a little ball and then sit with Steve to be petted and enjoy time together.

McPherson was a great friend—a dog that stuck closer than a brother. When he died he was over 12 years old. He had worked hard and played hard and taught us many life lessons. We all cried when we lost him. We still miss him to this day.

Arnold was a great friend too. He had been close to my parents and was a good buddy of mine until he died. Our families went camping together and spent many weekend evenings enjoying a barbecue and his favorite homemade ice cream.

Just before I got married he brought over a straw broom and dustpan. He handed them to me and said, "Connie, when Steve comes home I want you to always have these in your hands so he knows you have been cleaning the house." It was a joke—but it was also a sweet, loving gesture. He took the time to go to the store, buy these things, and drive 14 miles to my parents' home to give them to me. That was over 39 years ago, and is still a precious memory.

Arnold drove a big, beautiful 18-wheel truck. He worked hard all his life. After many years he had to give up truck driving. He decided to put this truck we all loved on the market. My family considered buying it, but none of us had the funds for such a large unneeded possession. Arnold talked about his truck until the day he died. In fact, the man who bought it brought it to Arnold's funeral so everyone could see it again. It had been to many antique truck shows and won many prizes.

Before Arnold's illness kept him at home, he and his wife, Salome, were in my Sunday school class. Talking to him and listening to his low, slow speech was so comforting after both my parents died. I knew through the years he always loved me unconditionally—just as McPherson had. Arnold mentored me in unconditional love and taught me to take life more slowly and with a smile.

McPherson and Arnold were both loyal, loving, and sincere, and I thank God that I could count them my friends and that both were part of my life.

God understands how important friends are and the Bible talks about it. Friends teach us, guide us, love us, and tell us when we go wrong. They come to our aid when we need help and listen when we need to be heard. Proverbs 18:24 says, "One who has unreliable friends soon comes to ruin, but there is a friend who sticks closer than a brother."

McPherson and Arnold were those kinds of friends. I will remember McPherson's non-condemning spirit and his always-loving attitude. I will remember Arnold's calming and soothing effect on my life and his always-sweet smile. My life is richer for knowing them both and they will always be in my heart.

A friend loves at all times (Proverbs 17:17).

Consider This:

Have you ever had a pet or human friend that stuck closer than a brother? What made your friendship special? How has this pet or person been there for you? What qualities do you treasure in this special friend? What have you learned that can make you a better friend yourself? What do you still need to work on?

Part II

Tales to Stretch Your Faith

🐾 **Jazzmin** 🐾

The Dog Not Chosen
God Works in Miraculous Ways

There are only two ways to live your life.
One is as though nothing is a miracle.
The other is as though everything is a miracle.
ALBERT EINSTEIN

Jazzmin was "the dog not chosen"...because she *was* chosen. Are you confused yet? Humanly speaking, you should be. But it was all part of God's perfect plan to place this dog in a very special family He desired to bless.

My dear friend Val is part of that family. She was the first to see Jazzmin. At the time she had a husband, three sons, one elderly Beagle, and a pet lizard. The two younger boys had been helping out at a woman's home, and her Rottweiler had had a litter. She offered them a puppy.

That was not the kind of dog Val felt would suit their family. For years, she'd had it in her head to get an Airedale terrier. But she and her husband were working for an urban ministry. Pricey dogs weren't in their missionary budget.

Then one day Val was at the pet store, buying food for the lizard. She was stunned to see an Airedale puppy there. Normally, such dogs weren't found in pet shops. The female puppy was between two and three months old and cost a thousand dollars. Val sensed that this dog was supposed to join her family—but no way could they pay that.

Val left the dog in the store—and prayed. It was early July. Time passed. The puppy didn't sell. The dog was growing…and the price was shrinking. Val kept checking. By late August, the Airedale's price had dropped to five hundred dollars. But it was still more than Val's family could manage. All this time, she'd continued to speak to the Lord about this puppy. Now she asked a salesperson what happened if a dog didn't sell. She was told that sometimes the dog was sent to their other store—and sometimes the pooch was simply given away.

Another week or two passed. The puppy still had no takers. Val went in and talked to the manager. She observed that the puppy was getting way too big for her cage. What would they let the dog go for?

To her shock, the manager told her she could have the dog for *99 dollars*! Val told the fellow to wrap her up. They gave the pup a bath and a bow and Val took Jazzmin home. She proved to be the perfect pet for Val's boys, and thirteen years later, Jazzmin is still a treasured member of the Parker family.

Val knows Jazzmin was an answer to prayer and a miracle gift from God. His miracles come in all different shapes and sizes. The one God did for a certain prophet in ancient Israel came in the shape of an ax head.

This man was part of a company of prophets-in-training. The famous prophet Elisha was their mentor. At a certain point, they felt they needed larger quarters to meet in, and with Elisha's blessing, they started on the task.

The building site was a spot by the River Jordan. As they were chopping down trees, one prophet's iron ax head fell into the river and sank. This poor man's heart must have sunk along with it. He cried out to Elisha that the tool had been borrowed.

We might not think that losing an ax head is any big deal. But this was an expensive item in those days. It's possible that in order to earn the funds to replace it, this fellow might have had to drop out of "prophet school."

Elisha's response was swift and sure. He knew he served a God of miracles. He asked his student to show him where the ax head sank. Second Kings 6:6-7 records what happened next: "Elisha cut a stick and threw it there, and made the iron float. 'Lift it out,' he said. Then the man reached out his hand and took it."

The same God who made iron float is still doing miracles today. He hasn't changed. Val knows it every time she looks at Jazzmin. But not everyone might have recognized that this dog's price was slashed by God's hand. In our culture, we are more prone to mislabel God's miracles "coincidences," or neglect to look for them at all.

Val and her family were twice blessed by the miracle of Jazzmin. They were blessed by the dog, and by the knowledge of God's love and care. Will you watch for His hand in your life, so His miracles can bless you too?

You are the God who performs miracles; you display your power among the peoples (Psalm 77:14).

Consider This:

How has God worked in miraculous ways in your life and family? How did this build your faith? Have you shared these miracles to encourage others? How might you be more alert to future miracles God might do for you?

The Beagle and the Bus
Come to God as Little Children

All children are artists. The problem is
how to remain an artist once he grows up.
PABLO PICASSO

One day when Alex was in elementary school, he opened the door to go outside to wait for the morning school bus. Hearing the familiar hinges creak, the family escape artist (also known as Pepper the Beagle) bolted out the door. Fortunately, Alex's family didn't live on a busy city street. Cornfields, not skyscrapers, surrounded their farmhouse in this rural part of Pennsylvania. There was a better chance of Pepper being hit by an Amish buggy than a speeding SUV.

Little Alex tried to give chase, but Pepper was long gone. As Alex's mom took him out to wait for the bus, Alex worried Pepper would never return. His mom tried to reassure him that dogs could instinctively find their way home, but she couldn't hide the fact that she was worried too. She didn't want to make promises she couldn't keep. It was up to God to bring Pepper home.

Alex said a prayer.

Then, off in the distance, Alex's big yellow school bus approached from around a bend. Alex could only make out the top half of the bus because the bottom half was hidden by acres of corn. The odd thing was, the bus was moving very slowly, literally crawling along the road.

Alex and his mom wondered what could be the matter. Did the bus have a flat tire? Was it in need of repair?

As the bus came around the bend, Alex and his mom did double double takes. There, in front of the bus, proudly leading it down the middle of the road was…their runaway Beagle! The pup was 100 percent resolute in holding her leadership position, and the bus driver made no effort to honk her away. As the bus neared, Alex could see the driver's expression—not a trace of irritation or impatience, just a bemused smile.

The bus pulled up to Alex's driveway. Pepper raced to the front door and went back inside the house. No biggie. Business as usual for Super Dog. This year lead a bus, next year, perhaps drag home a 747?

Alex felt he'd witnessed a miracle. His mom told him Pepper hadn't run away after all, but had taken the initiative to fetch the bus. As Alex rode to school that morning, he was beaming with pride. Other kids' dogs fetched slippers or newspapers, but his dog delivered a whole school bus loaded with children. How cool was that?

Alex was so impressed, he wrote an essay about the miraculous event in first grade. It was entitled, "Lending a Helping Paw." As a budding writer today, Alex remembers his piece about Pepper as his first serious literary work.

I teach screenwriting for a living. It's the art of writing vivid, succinct word pictures that tell a story. What struck me about Alex's memory of his Beagle and the school bus were the visuals. I can see the movie poster. Cornfields for as far as the eye can see. A big yellow school bus being led by a Beagle. Pepper strutting like the

Music Man leading a parade of 76 trombones. The theme is the big and powerful being humbled and schooled by the small and weak.

It's a familiar theme in the Bible and there are a lot of great stories to illustrate it. One such story finds Jesus with His disciples, engaged in serious discussion about who can get into the kingdom of heaven—when they are interrupted by a gaggle of eager parents hauling their children over so Jesus can bless them.

The disciples are bugged that their quality time with the Master is being interrupted by a bunch of noisy rugrats. After all, Jesus isn't some mall Santa and perhaps He was about to reveal a big secret about the kingdom of heaven.

Here's what the Bible says in Matthew 19:13-15 (NLT): "The disciples scolded the parents for bothering him. But Jesus said, 'Let the children come to me. Don't stop them! For the Kingdom of Heaven belongs to those who are like these children.' And he placed his hands on their heads and blessed them before he left."

I can imagine the egg dripping off the faces of the high and mighty disciples! All their years of learning and study, all the hundreds of hours they'd listened to Jesus, all the meditation and heartfelt prayers—all good but in a moment, turned upside down and inside out. Little children leading *them* to insights about the kingdom of heaven!

And Jesus wasn't merely instructing the disciples through book knowledge. He had personal experience in the matter of being a gifted child. On a family trip to Jerusalem to attend the Passover festival, 12-year-old Jesus was accidentally left behind by His parents. When they came back to look for Him, they didn't find Him at the local playground or in the ancient equivalent of a video game arcade—no, they found their adolescent boy in the temple, interacting with an assemblage of religious teachers and wise men. This "tween" wasn't twiddling His thumbs or daydreaming. The Bible says He was an active participant in the discussion: "Everyone who heard him was amazed at his understanding and his answers" (Luke 2:47).

If you want to know the deepest secrets about the kingdom of heaven you need to be like a little child. You need to have the mindset of a Beagle who believed she could fetch and lead a school bus. It is the power of innocence and meekness and utterly childlike faith.

Thank God for dogs and kids. Without them we'd have a much harder time figuring out the great and unsearchable mysteries of God.

And [Jesus] said: "Truly I tell you, unless you change and become like little children, you will never enter the kingdom of heaven" (Matthew 18:3).

Consider This:

Have you ever gotten a spiritual insight from a pet or child? What was it? How did it impact your life? How might you need to become more like a little child to walk more closely with God?

All Her Children
Trust Takes Time

Trust is letting go of needing to know all
the details before you open your heart.
ANONYMOUS

Becky knew a stray dog was living in the orchard across the road from her house. She watched the dog on her way back and forth from work. From time to time, she would see people try to lure the animal, but the stray would not be beckoned.

This went on for about a year. One day Becky threw some old muffins into the alfalfa field, thinking the birds would eat them. The next morning she looked out to see the stray dog eating the muffins. And that's where the real story begins.

It became Becky's mission to get this homeless canine to trust her. She took food out to the edge of her yard and left it for the dog. The animal eyed her very cautiously, and would not approach the food until Becky walked some distance away. But as the weeks passed, this dog began to trust her kind human friend a bit more. Becky didn't have to walk so far away for the dog to start eating. It took about two months, but finally the dog let Becky get close enough to pet her. This was how Becky discovered a tick and an infected cut on the dog's side. The dog let Becky clean her up and put medication on her wound. As her trust continued to grow, Becky's new canine pal started sleeping on her back porch. Becky named the dog Bonnie.

As their friendship grew, so did Bonnie's body. It was evident that she was pregnant as she began to take on "the look." At this point, she was still disappearing and showing up again. Suddenly, one day, Bonnie showed up skinny.

Becky asked Bonnie where the puppies were. To her amazement, Bonnie headed out to the fenced-in back lot. She crawled under a hole in the fence where Becky couldn't go. Becky told Bonnie she was going back to the house to get the key to the gate. Bonnie crawled back through the fence hole and accompanied her human.

After Becky opened the gate, Bonnie led her to an old boxcar from a train. It was being used for storage. Bonnie had dug a hole under the boxcar. That's where the puppies were.

It was remarkable. A few months before, this dog wouldn't come near Becky. Now she was leading Becky to her puppies! Becky got down on her stomach in the dirt and started fishing them out one paw or tail at a time. Eleven puppies later, she had the whole litter. She stuffed them all into her shirt and carried them to the safety of her back porch where she could supervise them more closely. They lived in a plastic swimming pool until they were big enough to roam the yard. Becky found homes for ten of them and kept Bonnie and her cutest puppy, Tess. The more Bonnie trusted her human, the more Becky could offer her. Their relationship grew into a wonderful bond. In fact, Bonnie would not leave Becky's side. She even slept next to her human's bed at night.

Becky's relationship with Bonnie taught her several great lessons about her relationship with God.

First, Becky was watching Bonnie and was concerned for her

well-being even before the dog was aware of her. God had His eyes on us even when we were not yet aware of Him.

Second, Bonnie's trust was shaky. She ate and ran away again. Still, every time she returned, Becky welcomed her. God continues to love and welcome those who come to Him with shaky trust and don't yet understand what an intimate relationship with Him holds.

Third, Becky was patient with Bonnie's fears. It took time for Bonnie to come close enough for Becky to remove the tick and treat her wound. God waits patiently for us to allow intimacy with Him so that He can bind up our wounds and remove the things that torment us.

Finally, by the time Bonnie's puppies were born, she was willing to trust these most precious possessions to her human. Becky gathered the puppies up and protected them better than Bonnie could. Even though it is ever so hard to release our children to the Lord, He knows how to protect them and grow them up far better than we do. But it is only through getting to know who He really is that we can trust Him enough to place their lives in His hands.

Bottom line: God gave Becky a glimpse of His patience with us and showed her why He wants us to be intimate with Him. She realized that the better we get to know God, the more He can give us.

Jesus said, "I have come that they may have life, and have it to the full" (John 10:10). But, like Bonnie, we must allow it. Becky shared that during this time, God began teaching her how very much like stray dogs we are in our relationship with Him. He has so much to offer us, but fear keeps us at a distance. We come in just close enough to snatch up the scraps of the abundant life and run away again.

Or we may be like a friend of mine who is still spiritually searching. He reads everything he can find on different religions but can't seem to accept that Jesus is the truth he's been seeking. He rummages the orchard of life, hoping to score a few old muffins, when he could be feasting on a wonderful relationship with Christ.

Proverbs 18:24 says, "There is a friend who sticks closer than a brother." Jesus wants to be such a friend to us. Will you let Him draw you close so He can touch and heal you?

> *But I trust in your unfailing love; my heart rejoices in your salvation (Psalm 13:5).*

Consider This:

Are you still rummaging the orchard of life to score a few old muffins, or are you in a growing relationship with Jesus Christ? What "ticks" has He removed? What wounds has He bound up? How does that encourage you to trust Him even more and put what's most precious to you in His hands?

Driving on Faith
What It Takes to Find the One

In faith there is enough light for those who want to believe and enough shadows to blind those who don't.

BLAISE PASCAL

Daniel's beloved Australian cattle dog mix (mixed with what he didn't know) recently passed away. Hannah had been a part of Daniel's family for 14 years. He was only six when they adopted her, so it's hard for Daniel to remember a time when Hannah wasn't there. If dogs were judged by their resumes, Hannah's wouldn't be exceptional. While she did come when called, she resisted learning tricks, not even mastering Basic Ball Fetching 101. But Hannah was unfailingly loyal to Daniel and his family. She loved them and they loved her. That made her the best dog in the world.

It was devastating when Hannah contracted Lyme disease from a tick bite, destroying the nerves in her legs. Daniel dreaded putting her down. He remembers cradling her face in his hands before he left for work that fateful morning and when he returned, she was just *gone*.

Hannah was greatly missed. The house was too quiet. No more tip-tap-tipping of her paws scampering over the hardwood floors.

They missed her familiar bark, even her doggie smell. Daniel, like the rest of his family, felt a dog-shaped hole in his life.

The family decided it was an emptiness that needed to be filled. The only question was—how? In a world with millions and millions of dogs, how does one find the *right* dog? A dog who could possibly take Hannah's place?

Daniel's family found Hannah by making weekly visits to the local Humane Society. Now, they could search for dogs on the Internet. The good news was, there were hundreds if not thousands of dogs to choose from without leaving the comfort of their living room. The bad news was, there were hundreds if not thousands of dogs to choose from. This led to a paralysis of indecision. They had to narrow the search. Everyone agreed on a puppy. Cute. Little. A fresh start.

As to the breed, Daniel's mom insisted on a mutt because she'd heard they generally live longer and are less susceptible to disease. She also wanted a girl.

The narrowing process continued. No hard-to-manage long hair that would shed everywhere. Not too big or too small. Nothing that could be mistaken for a horse…or a rat. The family researched the traits of various breeds. An easy-going disposition was a must. No high-maintenance diva dogs need apply.

It was hard work assembling this wish list, but even harder trying to *find* this pup. The family scoured online rescue sites like desperate singles in search of a soul mate. No matches. Then it occurred to Daniel that he and his brother would soon be away at college. How would a lone puppy keep itself occupied while Dad was at work and Mom was out running errands? Daniel insisted they get two dogs to keep each other company. His mom wasn't thrilled with double dog duty, but reluctantly agreed—with the stipulation that the duo be a boy and a girl. She believed two of the same sex would be hostile to each other.

So, *two* puppies who met all the specs, who would get along with each other and the family—impossible! But nothing's impossible with God, right? Eventually, a promising prospect arose: a big litter of Australian shepherd/Jack Russell terrier mixes. There was only one problem: the dogs were in North Carolina and Daniel and his family lived in Maryland—400 miles and a seven-hour drive away.

The puppy hunters weighed the options. That much time and energy just to get a pair of dogs? It would be an overnight trip with costly gas and hotel fees. And what if, when the family finally got there, they were the wrong puppies? Their photos were cute and the owner swore they were adorable little beasts. But used car salesmen and purveyors of puppies have been known to bend the truth. What if these pups were lemons? What if the seller was hoping to unload them on a desperate out-of-town family who had just driven seven hours and spent the night in a hotel? How could they *not* feel obligated to buy 'em?

Doubt-ridden, Daniel went back to the Internet. Surely, there must be a brother/sister set of puppies that met their criteria closer to home. But there wasn't. They discussed lowering their standards. Big longhairs? Two males? But this wasn't a decision to take lightly. Not just any Spot, Shep, or Fido could fill the Grand Canyon in their hearts left by Hannah.

Daniel searched obsessively until he developed a bad case of online-dog-profile-phobia. He was in despair the right dogs would ever turn up. It was time to give up—or get going to North Carolina.

The family loaded up the van and took a drive of faith down south. Expectations and worries were running high. Four hundred miles, seven hours, and one hotel later they met the puppies.

They were just as advertised. Active but not too rambunctious. Friendly and loving. Short-haired, not too big, not too small. The family named the girl Panda because she was white with black spots around her eyes. They named the boy Bear because he was black and…looked like a bear. They thought it would be fun to yell "Panda Bear!" and have both puppies come running.

Panda and Bear are being housebroken. Getting shots. Learning tricks. The house is no longer silent. Eight different paws tip-tap-tip on the floors. Barking fills the air—lots of it. Now at college, Daniel's pleased to hear the dogs are great pals and play happily in the backyard.

As to that Hannah-shaped hole in their hearts? Panda and Bear didn't fill that hole like cookie-cut forms. But they have become a part of this family in their own way. In doing so, they are the fulfillment of all the criteria Daniel and his family hoped for.

They are also an illustration of a thing called faith.

Hebrews 11:1 (NIrV) says faith is "being sure of what we hope for. It is being certain of what we do not see." Without faith, Daniel and his family would not have left the comfort of their living room to take that seven-hour drive from Maryland to North Carolina. This family of puppy seekers hoped in these two puppies without actually seeing them. They studied the puppies' pixelated images, read about them, and spoke with the owner on the phone. But without taking that drive of faith, those hoped-for puppies would never have become real to them as their own precious dogs.

Those seeking the Messiah also had a lot of specific criteria. In fact, there are over 300 Old Testament prophecies that pointed the way to the coming Savior. Here are just a few. It had to be a man from the line of David. Born in a not too big, not too small town called Bethlehem. Oh, yes. And one more thing.

"Therefore the Lord himself will give you a sign: The virgin will conceive and give birth to a son, and will call him Immanuel" (Isaiah 7:14).

Yikes! His mother had to be…*a virgin.*

Now if that doesn't make the One hard to find, what does? Can you imagine the stress it would have caused Daniel's family if they'd added "puppies born of a virgin" to their wish list?

It takes a bit more faith to find an immaculately conceived human than a couple of short-haired puppies that don't shed much. I mean, how does one actually find a perfect man who never sinned, who is the Son of God, who died and rose again from the dead, who can fill that eternity of emptiness in your broken heart and save you from eternal death and give you the gift of eternal life? Where do you find Someone like that? You can read about Him in the Bible, listen to His words on your MP3 player, hear sermons about Him, and get down on your knees and pray to this invisible God. But you can't see Him with your own eyes. You can't look out your back window and see your next-door neighbor Jesus walking across His swimming pool or rebuking a fig tree, causing it to instantly shrivel up and die.

So if you can't see Jesus, He's not real, right?

Not unless you take that drive of faith.

Unless you are willing to take a leap of faith and believe He's as real as Panda and Bear, you will never have an actual relationship with Him. And you may miss out on the greatest blessing ever bestowed on mankind: knowing God's love for *sure*.

And without faith it is impossible to please God, because anyone who comes to him must believe that he exists and that he rewards those who earnestly seek him (Hebrews 11:6).

Consider This:

Do you believe that Jesus exists? If so, how has your life changed since He filled that God-shaped hole? If not, have you checked out the Bible to learn about the One? Would you consider taking a drive of faith to find out whether He is as advertised?

Trust and Be on TV
God Has a Role for You

Wicked men obey from fear; good men, from love.
ARISTOTLE

Like so many other folks, I love dogs. I have dogs that I call my friends in several cities. They know me and run up to me so I can hug them when I see them. But there is a dog I adore that I have never actually met. He is a television star. His character name is Levi and he plays on an old television series called *Sue Thomas, F.B.Eye*. Sue is deaf, so Levi alerts her to important sounds in her world. He has been trained to help in this way, just like Seeing Eye dogs are trained to help the blind.

The dog Levi's real name is Jesse. When the show's creators were just starting to cast, Jesse came to audition for them in Thousand Oaks, California. The creators fell in love with Jesse right away and hired him. He could do practically anything. If he was asked to do a new trick, his trainer and master, Bryan, would work with him just a little, and he'd catch on.

It was easy to see that Jesse loved his master and would do anything to please him. Bryan liked it when the writers would put little bits in the script to show off Jesse's skills. For example, Bryan taught Jesse to touch the elevator button with his nose or paw by putting a piece of a treat in the button. Sue would tell Levi which floor they wanted, and he would touch the appropriate button with his nose or paw. This would make everyone in the elevator smile—Levi included.

When Deanne, the actress who played Sue, first met Jesse, she fell in love with him too. But she was concerned about how he'd be treated as a working animal. She didn't yet know Bryan. When she saw Bryan lying with Jesse on the studio floor between takes, she realized Jesse was loved and well cared for.

Joan Johnson, the writer and creative consultant, also remembers seeing Bryan and Jesse lying together. It was several years later, at the end of shooting the show. Bryan was stretched out on the floor with Jesse's head resting on his chest. Jesse was breathing more heavily now because he was older and had cancer. But the two of them rested peacefully together—dog and master.

Joan described Bryan as a tough guy. He was a stunt man, motorcyclist, and the alpha dog in his relationship with Jesse. But Jesse also knew Bryan loved him with all his heart, and the dog would do anything for his master. If Bryan was out of his sight, Jesse would turn his head to look for him. Though Bryan was tough, he was also very sweet, kind, and loyal. Jesse knew this and seemed to love Bryan with all his heart, mind, and spirit.

My Master is also strong and tough. He is not my alpha dog. He is the Alpha and Omega, the beginning and the end. When He tells me to do something, I wish I could say that I immediately jump up and do it. But I am not as obedient as Jesse. Sometimes it takes me longer to listen or act on my Master's commands.

This morning I took my father-in-law to the doctor's office. My mother-in-law comes along, so I usually don't go into the office. But today, I felt the Lord leading me to walk with them to the waiting room. This time I obeyed without hesitation. We sat down and had a nice chat. When his name was called, my in-laws both went into the examining room and I stayed behind.

Just as I was wondering why God had sent me there, I heard the voice of a dear old friend. I hadn't noticed she was sitting across the room. I walked over and we hugged and shared news of our families. I met her daughter and granddaughter. I had not seen this friend for several years, and during that time she'd developed cancer. She told me she'd decided to stop her chemotherapy. She said she didn't know how long she had on earth, but God was in charge. Through the sadness we found time to reminisce about some of our fun times with Moms in Touch and Youth for Christ, where we had both served as volunteers. If I had not obeyed my Master, I would not have had this precious, and perhaps final, visit with this dear old friend.

Back in Bible times, God asked Noah to play a starring role on the stage of history. He asked Noah to build an ark and put two of every living thing inside, along with himself and his whole family. The rains were coming to destroy the earth. Noah loved God, and he obeyed…even though the people around him didn't think the flood would ever happen. But God was as good as His word. The rains came. The ark floated. And when the waters receded, Noah and his family were safe and healthy.

I may not have the same role to play on God's stage as Noah or Jesse. But I want to play the part He has for me. Like Jesse, I love my Master with my whole heart, mind, soul, and strength. I know I can trust Him with my life and everyone and everything I know. Like Jesse, I seek my Master and His guidance. And after a long, busy day, I imagine myself laying my head on my Master's chest where I can rest with sweet abandon.

Love the Lord your God with all your heart and with all your soul and with all your mind and with all your strength (Mark 12:30).

Consider This:

What roles might God be calling you to play for Him on the stage of life? How can loving and obeying Him help you? Where are you finding it hard to do this? What Scriptures might encourage you?

Life Preserver with Paws
Will You Be God's Instrument?

*Faith is deliberate confidence in the character of God
whose ways you may not understand at the time.*

OSWALD CHAMBERS

B ogie was a marvelous female German shepherd who belonged
to the Allyn family. She was six or seven years old when she became
part of an amazing God-shaped miracle.

Bill and Penny Allyn were at their summer home in a small
upstate New York town. It was a beautiful cabin overlooking
a spring-fed lake. On this June day the water temperature was
chilly—probably 65 degrees or colder. They were cooking break-
fast for their youngest son, Mark, and some of his buddies. They
were also watching their two-year-old grandson, Noah.

Noah was right there with the rest of the family. Then, suddenly, they realized their grandson was gone. They raced outside
but didn't see him. Their immediate nightmare scenario was that
the toddler would wander into the lake and drown.

Bill called 911. He urged them to send help, including what was
needed for underwater rescue. Penny asked Mark and his friends
to start searching too. At some point, the family realized that Bogie

was also missing. This had never happened before. They had an electronic fence and their dog had never breached it—until now.

All these years later, memories differ. What the family does agree on is that Noah was missing for about 45 minutes. At some point, Mark spied Bogie from the end of the Allyn's dock—and possibly Noah too. They were some distance away, near the lake. Bill leaped into his car and raced to the spot. They also got a call from someone saying they had seen a toddler running with a German shepherd.

When Bill reached Bogie, she was standing between Noah and the water. Noah was throwing stones over Bogie's back. There was also a woman nearby who said she'd seen Bogie blocking Noah from going onto the docks.

There was more. To reach this location, boy and dog would have had to travel through a densely wooded and swampy area near the highway. There were deep gullies, and one spot where a plank was laid across a creek. This was a journey fraught with peril for a toddler. Bill and Penny believe Bogie must have guided Noah and kept him safe.

In the case of the Allyn family, God used a caring dog to protect and save a human child. In the case of Jews exiled to Persia many long centuries ago, God used an initially reluctant young woman to prevent a mass extermination.

The place was Persia. The time was the Babylonian captivity. The life preserver of God's choosing was a beautiful young Hebrew woman named Esther. Through a series of circumstances, the Persian king, Xerxes, chose Esther to be his new queen. However, he did not know that she was Jewish.

Haman, a high official at court, was plotting to have all the Jews in the kingdom killed. Esther's cousin, Mordecai, begged her to speak with the king. But at first she hesitated. If she went to the king without being summoned, she could be put to death. Mordecai responded with the now-famous words, "Do not think that because you are in the king's house you alone of all the Jews will escape. For if you remain silent at this time, relief and deliverance for the Jews will arise from another place, but you and your father's family will perish. And who knows but that you have come to your royal position for such a time as this?" (Esther 4:13-14).

Esther asked that the Jews fast and pray for her. She and her maids also fasted and prayed. God gave her favor with the king, the Jews were spared, and Haman was hanged.

I believe Bogie and Esther were both used by God for "such a time as this." I believe He has special things for each of us to do. In big and small ways, He calls all of us to minister to one another. He could choose to act directly, but instead He allows us the privilege of participating with Him. Will you pray and ask how He might choose to use you even today to be an instrument of His miracles and love?

For we are God's handiwork, created in Christ Jesus to do good works, which God prepared in advance for us to do (Ephesians 2:10).

Consider This:

Is there a person or pet God has used in a special, and perhaps surprising, way in your life? What happened? How did it bless you? How did it strengthen your faith? How might God want to use you in someone else's life today?

Dream Dog Guarantee
Take God at His Word

In God we trust. All others we virus scan.
ANONYMOUS

After many years as a bachelor, Chris longed to find the woman of his dreams. But with no soul mate on the horizon, he decided the next best thing was to find the dog of his dreams. Surely fear of commitment would be easier to overcome with a dog than with a lady. There wouldn't be a time-consuming and expensive dating process, either. He could just go online or cruise the local pet shops, check out all the doggies in the window, and pick one. That would be that.

Chris decided he'd go for a mutt—no fancy, high maintenance pup for him. He checked out the online site for the Pasadena Humane Society. Though he found a few cuties, when he went down to meet them in person he discovered they were already taken. Then, just as he was about to leave, a particularly unkempt dog caught his eye. It gave him such a friendly look that Chris had to stop. He knelt down and looked through the wire cage into this dog's eyes. They were kind and gentle, and Chris felt an instant connection. He wondered if his heart was saying, "This is your canine soul mate."

When Chris inquired about the dog, he learned she had a shattered hip, probably the result of being hit by a car. It had mended, but she had residual pain. For the rest of her life, this dog would walk with a limp and have to run on three legs.

Chris had a decision to make. Was this mangy, crippled stray the dog of his dreams? As he weighed the pros and cons, he felt the familiar fear of commitment creeping up his spine. What if he made the wrong choice? Luckily, this dog came with a warranty that eased his fear. The shelter workers told him that their dogs came with a guaranteed unconditional return policy. For as long as this dog lived, if things didn't work out for any reason, Chris could bring her back.

Chris had to wonder, with a chuckle, if he'd have married by then had the women he dated come with a guarantee like that. In the case of the dog, it tipped the scales. This shelter had a great reputation. People he knew had had positive dealings with them. Chris threw caution to the winds and brought the dog home.

That was a few years ago, and Chris and Luna turned out to be a perfect match. The lowly Cinderella dog proved to be a princess and, like in the fairy tale, these two are living happily ever after. As for Chris finding his dream woman—stay tuned!

I have also been emboldened to make decisions based on warranties from reliable guarantors. We often shop at a very popular membership warehouse store. Normally, I'd never buy pants or shirts without trying them on. But because friends and relatives have told me this store has an amazing no-questions-asked return policy, I recently grabbed up a pair of pants and some shirts and fearlessly tossed them straight into the shopping cart. Likewise, I purchased a previously-owned laptop online, sight unseen, from a total stranger because that seller offered an eBay-approved warranty.

That outfit's reputation and track record made me feel confident I would not get stuck with a laptop lemon.

Guarantees are only as good as the source that backs them. Would Chris have taken Luna home if her guarantee was given by a guy selling dogs out of his van? Would I buy pants at a swap meet and believe I could get a refund two months later if they didn't fit? Would I purchase a used laptop online because "Joe Private Party" assured me it was in perfect condition? No, no, no—because I'm afraid of making a wrong decision and I couldn't trust the credibility of those guarantors.

Choosing pets, pants, and laptops is one thing. But what about the larger decisions of life? In a different way from Chris, I faced the fear of making a wrong choice when I was deciding whether to marry my wife. I was in grad school getting my MFA in screenwriting. This is not exactly like getting a degree in brain surgery. Arts degrees often translate into a freelance lifestyle, meaning you're "free" from a regular paycheck and company health insurance. I had some fear about whether or not I could provide for Celine, and she did too. Luckily, we had a Guarantor of proven reliability we could turn to for reassurance—God.

Okay, so God didn't offer us a return policy on each other. Scripture says marriage is meant to be for life. But He did guarantee He would provide for us as His children. In Philippians 4:19, God promises that He will "meet all your needs according to the riches of his glory in Christ Jesus."

That lifetime guarantee from God greatly eased our fear about getting married. We believed that regardless of our job situation or the size of our bank account, God would meet our needs as long as we walked with Him. After 12 years, the ever-faithful Backer of that guarantee is still keeping His word.

Scripture is filled with many other marvelous eternal guarantees and promises God offers because of His great love for us. Who knows what fears we might shake off and what decisions we might dare to make if we learned those promises and took Him at His Word?

Not one of all the LORD's good promises to Israel failed; every one was fulfilled (Joshua 21:45).

Consider This:

Has a guarantee or warranty ever been a crucial factor in your decision-making? Did you have to use it? Was it honored? How has a promise of God helped you overcome fear and make a crucial choice?

Papillon Heaven Can Wait
God's Timing Is Perfect

Never be afraid to trust an unknown
future to a known God.
CORRIE TEN BOOM

For years and years, a sweet friend of mine dreamed of having a little black-and-white papillon puppy. Her boys had their pets as they were growing up, but the little papillon remained her unfulfilled longing.

When her youngest son graduated from high school, he also had a dream—to join the military. His dream would bring more challenges than hers. On July 4, 2001, he entered the U.S. Army's 82nd Airborne Trooper Division. On September 11, 2001, she knew where her son was headed. She waited and waited to hear from him. She wondered what he was thinking. How was he doing? Was he prepared?

Finally she got a letter in the mail. It read, in part: "Mom, please remember that I chose to be here. It is my honor and privilege to serve my country and protect the ones I love."

This young soldier's parents were overwhelmed with relief to hear from their son, and in awe of the courage he had. He had taken on the responsibility of a man. During the three years of his military service in Iraq and Afghanistan, my friend's life was consumed with prayer for him. Her concern was taking a toll and her zest for living had been smothered. Her husband saw that she needed a distraction. Maybe it was finally time to make her papillon puppy dream come true!

My friend's husband took her to a breeder's home. As they stood on the porch and knocked, they could hear several little barks from inside. When the breeder opened the door, my friend literally fell to her knees as 15 little papillon puppies swarmed excitedly around her. She was in love! They were so welcoming and happy as they jumped all over her. She was in papillon heaven!

How was she going to pick only one? Well, it finally came down to two. One was a very small black-and-white male, happy and full of energy. He was just like the puppy she had pictured all those years. The other was a timid, insecure, scared, constantly shaking little sable-and-white female.

My friend spent some time sitting on the kitchen floor with the puppies, trying to decide. All at once, the little female jumped into her lap. She let out a growl, declaring to her brother that this lady was her new master. That little puppy sealed the choice. It seemed that God had chosen them for each other. This puppy needed love, and my friend had an abundance of love to give.

With her sons grown, my friend had felt an emptiness inside. She had always wanted a papillon puppy, but the need for one grew in her heart as concern for her son robbed her of her joy in life. She understood that a puppy wasn't the answer to all her problems. She knew Jesus as her personal Savior and realized that He was the One who had filled the spiritual hole in her life many years before. But Jesus knew of her desire and I believe it was His timing to bless her in this way. Her husband also knew about her dream, and wanted to make it a reality and see his beautiful wife smile again. When she couldn't decide which puppy to pick, a puppy decided for her. I believe that God had chosen just the right puppy and this was His way to delight her.

The match was perfect! Isabella, the beautiful papillon, lived in luxury at her new home. She spent hours sitting on my friend's lap. My friend's tired heart grew fresh once again. Her smile came back and she had a lighter step in everything she did. She thanked God for her little puppy and gave Him the glory when her son came home safely from proudly serving his country.

Although she had wanted this puppy for many years, God gave her the dog in His time. He also brought me this story in His time. Even though this particular friend lives less than a mile from me, we never seem to get together. But one day not long ago, she emailed me and we decided to have lunch. We had a wonderful time and I told her about this book. She shared her puppy story with me. Had the timing of our lunch been different, I know I would have loved hearing the tale, but it might not have found its way into these pages.

God's puppy timing in my friend's life was perfect, even though she felt she'd had to wait a long time. The same was true for a biblical character named Joseph. He was a Hebrew whose jealous brothers had sold him into slavery in Egypt. He had been falsely accused and wound up in prison. After a time, two of Pharaoh's officials wound up in the prison too. Joseph interpreted their dreams correctly. When one of them, the cupbearer, was freed, Joseph begged the man to remember him to Egypt's ruler. But the cupbearer forgot Joseph for two full years—until Pharaoh himself had troubling dreams that no one understood. Then the cupbearer recalled how Joseph had interpreted his dream. Joseph was brought to the Egyptian ruler, successfully interpreted a dream that foretold a famine, and became second-in-command to Pharaoh himself. Joseph was used by God to preserve not just Egypt, but his own Hebrew family in the time of famine.

God knew just when Joseph needed to be brought to Pharaoh's attention. He knew just when my friend needed a little bundle of papillon joy! And we can trust that His timing is perfect in our lives as well, because He is infinitely wiser than we are and He loves us!

I remain confident of this: I will see the goodness of the LORD in the land of the living. Wait for the LORD; be strong and take heart and wait for the LORD (Psalm 27:13-14).

Consider This:

Have there been instances in your life when God's timing was different than yours? What happened? How did you see His wisdom? How has that strengthened your faith in His love and care?

The Appointed Time

Our Lives Are in God's Hands

*There is a time for everything, and a season
for every activity under the heavens.*

ECCLESIASTES 3:1

Nancy's dog Rascal could've been a furry stuffed animal. He was
that cute. With his soft, fuzzy coat and warm teddy bear eyes, he
was impossible not to hug. Even people who disliked dogs were
disarmed by his charm and playful personality.

Rascal's name fit him to a tee when he was a puppy—simul-
taneously sweet and rambunctious. As he aged he never lost his
sweet spirit, but physically he began to slow down. First came the
arthritis. Rascal would pull himself along on his front legs, pain-
fully dragging his stricken hind legs behind him. Nancy put special booties on his feet so he wouldn't rip open his claws and bleed.

Then came the cataracts that dimmed his vision. When it got
dark outside, Nancy turned on the bright pool lights so he could
navigate by seeing the shadows. The family became extra vigilant
because Rascal had stumbled into the pool a few times and had
needed to be rescued. Even their new puppy was keeping a watchful

eye. Nancy would occasionally witness the little dog blocking Rascal's errant path and steering him away from the pool.

Rascal became incontinent. He couldn't control his bladder. Instead of going out to the backyard, he'd stagger to his feet and relieve himself in the den. Nancy switched his sleeping quarters from the living room to the laundry room, where the floor was tile.

About this time, Nancy's husband and eldest son broached the subject of putting Rascal down. But Nancy wouldn't have it. She knew in her heart it wasn't time. Rascal still greeted her with a smile and wagged his tail when she patted his head. His body may have been weak but his spirit was alive and well. So what if dear Rascal occasionally wet the floor? That's not a sin punishable by death! Nancy wondered how her loved ones would treat her if she were in Rascal's shoes. "The first time I need Depends, I'm out the door, huh?" she joked.

Rascal lost control of his bowels next. As he began to regularly soil himself, Nancy and her husband would wake up extra early before going to work to bathe him. It was becoming more and more time-consuming and stressful to care for their rapidly deteriorating pet. Still, Nancy would not entertain the thought of ending Rascal's life.

She just knew it wasn't time.

Rascal still enjoyed his meals. He did his best to play with the puppy, albeit only for a few seconds before tiring. And whenever Nancy held Rascal close, she experienced the same loving warmth that bonded them the first time she held him as a puppy. No matter what anyone else said, she knew Rascal wasn't ready to go.

Then, on a certain Friday in October that Nancy will never forget, things changed.

Nancy came downstairs in the morning to find Rascal whimpering. The sound cut Nancy like a knife. Not once in Rascal's

16-and-a-half years had she ever heard him cry. Nancy's heart broke and the tears came.

She knew it was time.

Rascal's medications could no longer suppress the pain. Nancy could handle the extreme caregiving, but not Rascal suffering. She found it difficult to sleep that night. At work the next day, she couldn't get Rascal off her mind. When she got home, Nancy called the vet. Through tears, she told the woman on the phone that she thought she and Rascal were ready. The compassionate voice on the line assured her the doctor would be available tomorrow and that if Nancy changed her mind, it would be okay.

Nancy sat alone with Rascal, wanting to be sure beyond a shadow of a doubt that she was making the right decision. She had 12 hours to change her mind. Nancy desperately wanted someone to talk to. At that moment, a good friend dropped by. As they spoke about Rascal, he began to whimper and moan. It was further confirmation. Then, Nancy's youngest son came home. She asked what he thought about Rascal. Up to now, he had never voiced an opinion. He took a moment, then said, "Mom, it's time."

That night, the family gathered around Rascal. Nancy got down on the floor and lay beside him, holding him in her arms. As they all said their good-byes, Nancy recalled something she had read in a devotional: "Let go, let God." She realized the power of life and death ultimately lay in God's hands.

Nancy let go.

She and her husband brought Rascal to the vet in the morning. Rascal didn't go down as quickly as planned. His breathing slowed, his head flopped down, but his heart kept on beating. It was as if he was trying to hang on just a little longer. Maybe Nancy was ready to let go, but what if Rascal wasn't?

Nancy leaned down and whispered in his ear that she loved him, that she would miss him greatly, and that she would always remember him. She assured him it was okay to go because she would be all right. Rascal took a final breath and let go.

From that moment on, Nancy has felt only peace. Even through sadness and tears, not once has she doubted her decision. If she had allowed Rascal to linger on and suffer, she's sure this peace would have eluded her.

"Let go, let God" was the key. When Nancy acknowledged God was infinitely more qualified than she in matters of life and death, she knew His timing was perfect. Ecclesiastes 3:1-2 (NASB) tells us, "There is an appointed time for everything...A time to give birth and a time to die."

When I thought about how much consideration and heart went into Nancy's decision as to the appointed time for Rascal, it got me thinking about how much consideration and heart goes into God's decisions concerning our appointed times.

Actually it's unfathomable. It's beyond my wildest comprehension. I don't know the words that can remotely touch how God must feel about setting the appointed times for all living creatures, past, present and future—including you and me.

Nancy had to deal with one beloved dog.

God has dealt with untold billions of human beings over countless centuries. Every one of these lives and deaths are as individual as snowflakes, no two alike, each with an infinite number of possibilities. But we all share one thing in common: We all have a time to die.

The only question is...when?

Genesis 5:27 tells us, "Methuselah lived a total of 969 years, and then he died." God's appointed time for this Old Testament guy was nearly a millenium.

Matthew 2:16 reveals the opposite end of the spectrum. "When Herod realized that he had been outwitted by the Magi, he was furious, and he gave orders to kill all the boys in Bethlehem and its vicinity who were two years old and under." For those little boys, their appointed time was less than two years. That seems terribly wrong. Who in their right mind would decide that two years is the appointed time for any human being?

But the Bible says God cares about us more than sparrows and lilies of the field. This may be controversial for some dog lovers, but I think God loves us even *more* than we love our dogs. Yes, that much. As Nancy let go and let God with regards to Rascal, the same comfort and peace is available to you and me in our times of loss and grieving. And it's always good to remember to Whom we're letting go. Not a cold and distant God who doles out appointed times like a heartless lottery machine, but a God who dwells so close we can feel His very presence.

Our God resides in our hearts.

Our God is the very same God who sent His precious only Son to die on the cross at an appointed time...for *us*.

God is mysterious. His ways and thoughts are higher than ours. God is love. And in that love is the greatest reason why we should let go and let Him. You may have heard it a million times. You may have memorized it in Sunday school when you were little. But have you visited it lately? It's the marvelous promise found in John 3:16.

For God so loved the world that he gave his one and only Son, that whoever believes in him shall not perish but have eternal life (John 3:16).

Consider This:

Have you ever wrestled with losing a beloved pet or person? Were you able to let go and let God? If so, what difference did that make? If not, would you be willing to let go and let God right now?

Scary Larry
Fear Makes Monsters

The only thing we have to fear is fear itself.
FRANKLIN D. ROOSEVELT

When a young couple moved in next door we met the new neighbors, but not their dog. Visiting them was not that easy, because they were very busy. They were fixing up their beautiful home and large yard with a pool, guesthouse, and horse facilities. They both had demanding jobs as well.

I wasn't sure what all their pets were, but I was aware of their large, frightening dog. I hadn't seen him, but I had heard his huge, bellowing bark. I was just sure that if our little Squitchey got in his way, he could gobble her up in one bite. And when we had a big rain, I knew Squitchey would have an easy job of digging her way under the fence until my husband, Steve, could repair each soft place with rocks.

One day Squitchey heard the man next door working on his yard. She didn't know the property boundaries and was out to protect her family. She dug her way under the fence and barked furiously at him with all seven pounds of her spirited little body. Steve heard the ruckus and ran out to save the neighbor. I figured if the man's dog had been with him, Squitchey would have more than met her match—which made me all the more nervous about this "monster." Every time Scary Larry (as I had nicknamed him) barked, I felt compelled to check our backyard for Squitchey to make sure she had not become his next meal.

Finally, I decided that I had been afraid long enough. It was time to meet this beast and see if my imagination was bigger than the dog himself. I wrapped up some homemade cookies and walked over.

Jenna, the wife, came driving home just as I arrived. We met at the front door and I gave her the cookies and asked to meet her dog. She wanted to know which one. So now I found out there were two beasts living next door to me! I said I'd like to meet them both. She led me to the backyard and there, behind a fence, were the beasts—not Scary Larry, but Buddy and Belle. Belle was a beautiful white Lab. She was as sweet as could be, and I would have liked to go behind the fence and pet her. But the other beast, Buddy the Dalmatian, didn't give me quite as warm a welcome as Belle did. He growled and barked and showed his teeth—but Jenna assured me that he would not attack. I talked to both of them and Buddy settled down a bit. Maybe next time I'll go behind the fence and get to know them better. I do feel confident that one day soon we will all be friends.

Scary Larry the monster dog wasn't real. He was a figment of my fears. He didn't live anywhere but in my head. Now I have a confession to make. Many years ago I gave a young schoolboy a "Scary Larry" type of fright by pretending to be a monster myself.

I was 19 years old and traveling with a professional Christian music group. We were touring one of England's many castles. It was more in ruins than many of the others. I loved standing away from the group, pretending I was royalty and was in the market for a castle to buy.

It was a cool day and I was wearing a dark brown coat with white fur on the collar and cuffs. My tour group went ahead of me as I stayed behind to check out the kitchen. It had a huge cave-like oven big enough to hold several people. It was dark in the castle and even darker in the oven. I heard a group of schoolchildren coming and decided to have some fun. I crawled way into the back of the oven, put my arms around my face, and sat quietly until the children arrived.

One curious little boy slowly walked to the face of the oven. I began to move my arms a bit. He alerted his teacher that something was in the oven. His teacher didn't sound too concerned, probably assuming the boy's imagination was running away with him. She called him over to her—but he crept closer to me. So I made a low growling noise. The boy screamed and took off. I squelched my giggles and sat quietly until they all left. It was ornery of me, but it sure was fun. I owe that little boy an apology. I'm sure he thought he was going to be a beast's lunch that day.

Not all our fear monsters are pretend. Some of them are rooted in reality. Recently I have been dealing with the fear of dying. I'm not afraid of dying, really, because I know I will be in heaven with my Savior. I just don't want to leave my husband or the rest of my family yet. This beast of fear is no idle worry. Three years ago I underwent a quadruple bypass, and not long ago I spent four days in the hospital with another heart problem. I had several major tests, including an angiogram. Steve stayed with me and our daughter Christy came to visit but couldn't bear to watch me being taken by gurney to the examining room. The doctors found a blocked artery they've been able to treat with medication.

I believe the beast called Satan has been using my health concerns to growl at me, putting unnecessary fear in my life. But I don't have to let him make this monster bigger than it is. God reminds me in His Word that He is in control. According to Psalm 139:16,

"All the days ordained for me were written in [God's] book before one of them came to be." He knew the days of my life long before I was born. I am in His hands.

Scary Larry—that is, Buddy—is not going to eat Squitchey. He's a good dog. He was only a beast of my imagination. Satan is very real, but my Savior is protecting me from him. God is in charge.

I am learning once again that monster fear is not from God. So I think I'll go over and visit my new friends Buddy and Belle.

I sought the LORD, and he answered me; he delivered me from all my fears (Psalm 34:4).

Consider This:

Has fear created any monsters in your life? What are they? What makes them so scary? Which are imaginary and which are rooted in reality? Which Scriptures might cut them down to size and remind you that God is bigger?

A Time to Wean
God Grows His Children

*You have to do your own growing no
matter how tall your grandfather was.*
ABRAHAM LINCOLN

Some young friends of mine are in Scotland right now with their two small sons. Dan shared a marvelous story today. It was too windy for his three-year-old to walk down the hill from preschool. When he asked Jayden if he wanted Daddy to carry him a little, the child answered, "I want you to carry me a lot!"

When I first got my dog Munchie, he wanted me to stay with him a lot—as in, every single minute!

Munchie had been a beloved pet whose owner could no longer care for him. He was put in a shelter, and then rescued. For a while, he lived in a desert-area foster home. But it wasn't meeting his needs, so I agreed to take him.

Munchie was brought to me in the evening. I already had three other dogs. Because he was new, and because I wasn't too sure about his bathroom habits, I decided to keep him by himself in my office overnight. Munchie decided otherwise. He whined and whined until I gave in and let him join his new pack on my bed so I could get some sleep.

Next morning, I took him back to my office along with the rest of my pups. That was fine—until I went to leave the room. He launched a full-scale doggie protest, howling and scratching at the door. Clearly he'd lost one too many humans and didn't want me to leave his presence. Talk about separation anxiety!

I realized Munchie needed to be weaned of this clinginess in short order or I'd feel like I had a four-legged Siamese twin. Okay, maybe I exaggerate, but I couldn't live this way! Fortunately, I remembered what a trainer had once told me. He'd suggested that leaving a dog alone for brief periods and then returning could help condition the dog to be without me. I decided to go and come frequently from that office so Munchie would see that he wasn't being abandoned. After doing this for a couple of days, he got the memo and calmed down.

If Munchie had spoken English and was capable of expressing his feelings, he probably would have rejected my game plan. He might not have felt at all ready to be "weaned." But as his loving new dog mom, I trusted my choice over his. In short order, my decision was confirmed by his adjustment.

There was a point in my life when I, too, needed to be weaned of excessive dependence on a key person in my life. In my twenties, I accepted a job with an uncle's nonprofit health organization. My task was to write a weekly column on health and wellness that we gave away to various newspapers. I was learning on my feet. But my dad was an experienced writer who had done extensive reading in the health arena. He became my go-to person. I would read my articles to him on the phone, and he would spot potential problems and flag them. I became extremely dependent on him for this assistance.

Finally, my dad decided that I needed to be "weaned." He sensed that part of me resented my dependence on him. He thought I'd done my job long enough to have some decent judgment of my own. But like Munchie all those years later, I resisted.

Then Dad got cancer.

Suddenly, depending on Dad was no longer an option. But the weaning didn't stop there. I had two colleagues I relied on as well. One left the organization. The other was in a freak accident that caused her to be unavailable to me for many weeks.

Humanly, I was howling and scratching at the door. But I had not been abandoned. I knew Jesus, and He was right there with me. Looking back, He was doing a work in me, growing and stretching me in ways I would not have chosen for myself. Ultimately, my dad passed away, but I kept writing and grew personally and professionally from the experience.

Jesus's disciples also went through a difficult weaning process. They had gotten used to His physical presence. But the time had come for Him to go to the cross. He told them He wouldn't be with them much longer and was going where they couldn't come (John 13:33). They didn't like this, especially Peter. Peter howled and scratched at the door. He asked his Lord, "Why can't I follow you now? I will lay down my life for you" (John 13:37).

Jesus knew better. He knew Peter would deny Him. He also knew He wouldn't abandon Peter. Peter wasn't being forsaken; he was being refined and stretched and prepared for leadership.

Munchie is a happy, confident dog whose horizons have been greatly expanded by not needing to be joined at the hip to me. After Dad's death, I went on to write animated TV shows and books like this one. And though Peter initially denied his Lord, he was restored and went on to preach at Pentecost and assume a key leadership role in the early church.

Our loving heavenly Father knows just when and how we need to be weaned. He knows just when we are ready to take the next step. And He promises to be right there with us in that process. So when God beckons you out of your comfort zone, don't howl—embrace the new adventure!

But very truly I tell you, it is for your good that I am going away. Unless I go away, the Advocate will not come to you; but if I go, I will send him to you (John 16:7).

Consider This:

Has God ever called you to be weaned in a way you didn't feel ready for? How did you respond? What was the result? What did you learn that might encourage someone else who is in a weaning process?

Now You See Her, Now You Don't

Believing Is Seeing

Faith is to believe what you do not see;
the reward of this faith is to see what you believe.
St. Augustine

When Meaghan first started learning tae kwon do at the tender age of seven, her dad told her she could have the dog she yearned for—once she earned her black belt.

Meaghan stretched, kicked, and punched her way to puppy ownership. She went to a number of breeders, saw a lot of dogs, but Max the tiny Yorkie towered above all the rest.

They became inseparable friends. When Max was little she brought him to visit her dad for a weekend. She had a babysitting job that night and was gone for many hours. When she returned, she found Max curled up on her sweatshirt. Max had recognized Meaghan's scent on the shirt and refused to move until she came back.

Max didn't have separation anxiety issues when Meaghan popped out on short errands to the store or even when she spent the day at school. He knew she'd be back in a reasonable period of time. But after years of childhood bonding and daily routine, it came time for Meaghan to go off to college. She would be absent for much longer periods of time than a babysitting job or a day in high school—and Max always knew.

He would sit on the stair-step he always sat on and sadly watch as Meaghan put her bags by the front door. When Meaghan tried to say good-bye, Max would turn away. He couldn't look at her. Meaghan finally had to take Max's face in her hands to give him a hug and a kiss. A few minutes later, Meaghan's mom would call to tell her that as soon as she left, Max broke from his perch and rushed to the window to watch her drive off. He'd stay at that window, staring out, long after the car was gone. Did he feel abandoned? Was he anxious and fearful that she might never return? Or was he simply blue because he knew she'd be away for many a moon?

We can't be sure what dogs are thinking, but we know what people think. We've all felt sad when a loved one was going away for a long time, whether it was off to college a few hours from home or a job transfer to the far side of the world. The first time my wife and I dropped our three-year-old son off at preschool, we saw a look of disorientation, then tears trickling down his face as we "abandoned" him to strangers. We knew he felt unsure if we would ever come back to get him. Or if we did return, would it be weeks, months, even years? However, when we did return for him that afternoon and every subsequent day he was dropped off, he began to gain confidence we would come back soon—just as Max felt comfortable that Meaghan would come back soon from a short errand or a day in high school. Both my son and Max were building a certain spiritual muscle necessary to believe that the one leaving would return. The stronger the muscle, the stronger the belief. This muscle is called faith.

It takes faith to believe in something you cannot see. When Max was peering out the window with that sad look on his face, it was impossible to test the strength of his faith. When Meaghan was going to be away a long time, was Max a dog of little or much faith? Was he wondering if she'd ever come back or did he strongly expect her return? It's open to speculation.

An interesting spin on believing or not believing in what you can't see is the concept of object permanence, a term coined by famous developmental psychologist Jean Piaget. Object permanence is a form of faith that develops in infants between eight and nine months of age. Before this time, most babies perceive the world in "out of sight, out of mind" terms. That is, if Mommy or Daddy leaves the room, the three-month-old has no idea if they still exist or if they're ever coming back. In the game of peekaboo, first you're there, then you hide behind a blankie and you're gone! Just as Baby gets anxious, you whip the blankie away and Baby giggles with delight that you're back from limbo.

Object permanence is that developmental milestone which makes a child no longer "fun" to play peekaboo with—when they believe that a person or object still exists even though that person or thing can't be seen. Or to say it another way, their faith muscle has grown strong enough to hold on to the reality of Mom or Dad even though they're not in the same room.

Faith in Jesus is a developmental milestone for those who profess to be Christians—or as some call themselves, believers. Christians are people with strong enough faith muscles to believe in Jesus even though He's not in the same room or even on the same physical planet. And as if that's not enough heavy lifting to strain our faith muscles, we also must believe in the Son of God even though we've never actually seen or touched Him.

At least Max actually got a kiss from Meaghan before she vanished off to college. And how crazy would it be to expect Baby to believe in Mommy and Daddy if Baby had never actually seen or touched them?

But that is exactly what we believers are called to do: have faith muscles of the buffest kind. We must be the spiritual counterparts of those big grunting Olympic power lifters. We need more faith than a Yorkie waiting for its master's return from college. More faith than a three-year-old waiting for Mommy to pick him up from preschool.

Does that seem unfair? Ridiculously difficult? Are we at a disadvantage compared to all those first-century believers who actually saw their Lord and Savior in the flesh? And what about Mary Magdalene and the disciples who not only walked and talked with Jesus while He was alive—but had the privilege of seeing Him resurrected a short time after He was crucified? It'd be a lot easier to believe in Jesus—and His eventual return—if we had had a few of those seeing-is-believing experiences.

But we haven't. It's been 2,000 years since Jesus last walked the earth. No one alive on planet Earth has ever seen Him or talked to Him, broken bread with Him, or hugged Him. But we're not at a disadvantage. If we can still believe in the object permanence of Christ under our present circumstances, we are not at a disadvantage at all. In reality, we're blessed! We have the opportunity to find God's favor in a very special way.

Take a look at the story of a disciple of Jesus who didn't catch on to the concept of object permanence the first time around. He obviously needed to get off the couch and work out more in the faith gym. This scene takes place after Jesus had risen from the dead.

> Now Thomas (also known as Didymus), one of the Twelve, was not with the disciples when Jesus came. So the other disciples told him, "We have seen the Lord!" But he said to them, "Unless I see the nail marks in his hands and put my finger where the nails were, and put my hand into his side, I will not believe." A week later his disciples were in the house again, and Thomas was with

them. Though the doors were locked, Jesus came and stood among them and said, "Peace be with you!" Then he said to Thomas, "Put your finger here; see my hands. Reach out your hand and put it into my side. Stop doubting and believe." Thomas said to him, "My Lord and my God!" Then Jesus told him, "Because you have seen me, you have believed; blessed are those who have not seen and yet have believed" (John 20:24-29).

Blessed are we who live in the twenty-first century. Blessed are we who have not seen Jesus and yet believe. Blessed are we who wait eagerly for our Lord and Savior.

The LORD is good to those who wait for Him (Lamentations 3:25 NKJV).

Consider This:

How has God strengthened your faith muscle to grow your trust in Him? What else might He be asking you to believe without first seeing? How have you been blessed by your faith?

And the Dog Came Back
Surrender Your Wish List

*Commit every particle of your being in all
things, down to the smallest details of your
life, eagerly and with perfect trust to the
unfailing and most sure providence of God.*
JEAN-PIERRE DE CAUSSADE

When my beloved Biscuit and Morgan were well into their senior years, I began thinking of adding to my canine family. I had a younger dog, a little Pomeranian named Becca. She was not quite six years old, and I thought a boy dog anywhere from about one to four years of age would be a perfect playmate. I began checking a popular pet adoption website and soon found a pooch that seemed a great possibility.

I made contact with the rescue group that had this dog. He was in foster care. Angie, the head of the group, was away on vacation. But she talked with me by phone. She thought someone might already be interested in the dog I had chosen. But she had another wonderful pup that might just suit my situation. She emailed a photo of an adorable papillon mix—and I fell in love. As we continued to communicate, it turned out both dogs might be available, and I emailed asking to meet each of them.

I had a hesitation, though. I lived in the city of Los Angeles. There was a legal limit of three dogs per household. I had rationalized that I wouldn't have four dogs very long. After all, my oldest was 15 and had a heart murmur that required medication. But even so, I was breaking the rules, wasn't I? When I called local animal control to ask if the regulations had changed, my guilt was reinforced. I decided I was doing the wrong thing. Scripture urges us to obey the laws of the land. I left a message for Angie that I'd had second thoughts. I especially hated to lose out on that papillon mix, but I surrendered him to God.

Little did I know how quickly God would give him back. I got a message from Angie a few days later. She had returned and found both my request to meet the dogs and my message backing off at the same time. She wasn't quite sure what I wanted to do. When I phoned to clarify, she had just been to visit the papillon mix in foster care. He was not in the best of shape. He had skin issues, and seemed miserable in his foster home's desert heat. She pleaded with me to take him on a temporary basis. She had no one else to care for him. She'd just prayed for a solution. Somehow it seemed the right thing to do. I agreed.

I didn't know, but God knew, that within a month I would lose the younger of my two senior pooches. I adopted the papillon mix I named Munchie. He proved older than we'd thought (eight years of age instead of four), but it didn't matter. He was clearly meant for me—a special gift from God. He and Becca get along famously, and Munchie is perfect for my home and a joy in every way.

God asked me to surrender a dog. He asked Israel's King David to surrender a building project. David longed to build a temple where God would dwell. God said no to that fond wish because David's reign had been filled with war and bloodshed. God ordered that the project be deferred to David's son Solomon, who would enjoy a reign of rest and peace. David laid his desire on God's altar and obediently prepared the way for Solomon to erect Israel's first temple.

I love Munchie, but I love God more. Nothing else I could want holds a candle to Him. I also realize that like King David, I don't always know what's best, so I lay my desires before the One who does.

> *Take delight in the* LORD, *and he will give you the desires of your heart. Commit your way to the* LORD; *trust in him and he will do this (Psalm 37:4-5).*

Consider This:

Have you ever surrendered a deep desire to the Lord? How did it affect your faith? What is hardest for you to surrender now? What might help you do so?

I Am the Tailgate

Enter In

*Indeed, it is easier for a camel to go through
the eye of a needle than for someone who
is rich to enter the kingdom of God.*

LUKE 18:25

It was summer of '76, Southern California—a scene out of a Beach Boys song.

Mark and his buddies were jammed into an old station wagon, surfboards lashed on top, radio blasting, heading back home from a long day of catching rays and waves. As Mark cruised through the remote coastal area, out of the corner of his eye he saw a huge odd-looking dog limping along the road. Mark wondered what a dog was doing way out here in the middle of nowhere. He slowed down and focused on this beast. It was more shadow than substance, a walking skeleton. Only it wasn't Halloween.

As Mark stared out the window, his friends knew him well enough to read his mind. Someone in the backseat laughed and shouted, "Don't pick it up; it's a devil dog!"

Indeed, the "devil dog" was a frightening sight. It was the size of a small horse and jet black—or covered with so much grime it appeared to be black. Its body was twisted and bent, its spine arched in a painful *C* like a canine hunchback—perhaps the result of a recent accident. As to this monster's breed, it appeared to be a Great Dane/black Lab misfire or a hideous reject from the laboratory of Dr. Frankenstein.

In the eyes of Mark's surfing companions, this dog was a totally worthless untouchable, a four-legged leper of the lowest canine caste. When Mark passed the dog, his pals breathed a sigh of relief. Mark wasn't that crazy after all. Then Mark pulled a U-turn and came up behind the devil dog. Mark *was* that crazy.

He got out and approached the dog. It turned to face him. This was the moment of truth. Would the poor downtrodden animal accept Mark's kindness? Or would the devil dog use its last gasp of strength to tear out Mark's throat?

Mark's friends watched from the safety of the station wagon. Without taking his eyes off the dog, Mark slowly opened the station wagon's tailgate. The next moment seemed like an eternity. Then, the dog wagged its tail. It was a barely perceptible wag—as if to wag any more would knock this poor animal over. Without hesitation, the beast staggered toward the open tailgate. This dog accepted Mark's invitation—no questions asked, no second thoughts.

When Mark reached down to lift the dog in, he almost threw the animal over his head. This dog felt hollow! It was skin and bones draped over a balsa wood frame. Mark realized it was probably hours from starving to death.

Once inside the car, the dog collapsed. It couldn't move a muscle. Mark dropped his eye-rolling friends off and took the dog home. His sister was visiting with her own dog, a young female in heat. Mark's dog, a male, even though close to death, perked up in the presence of this girlie pooch. Mark saw the twinkle in his new dog's eye and knew his skeletal pal would pull through just fine.

Mark named the dog Big Sid. He weighed 45 pounds when

Mark rescued him. After eating like a horse for a couple of months, the dog doubled his weight. Mark kept him for two very happy years, until Big Sid finally contracted cancer and had to be put down. Mark fondly remembers Big Sid as the most appreciative dog he's ever owned. Big Sid never lost his attitude of gratitude.

This is a story that could raise a number of interesting questions. But I always wondered why Mark stopped to open the tailgate. And once he did, why did Big Sid come without hesitation?

Mark said he felt "prompted in his spirit" to stop the car. He'd seen many stray animals—but he felt a special connection with this particular lost and broken dog. He wasn't sure what would happen. He only knew he was supposed to open the tailgate. Then it was up to the dog. Mark wouldn't grab the dog or tempt it with food. He wouldn't call to it or do anything to force it to get into his car. But if it chose to come forward on its own, Mark knew the dog was his.

This story illustrates a great biblical truth. Jesus says in John 10:9, "I am the gate; whoever enters through me will be saved."

That's pretty clear. If you want to be saved and spend eternity in heaven, you have to enter through a gate named Jesus. Jesus doesn't go out and yank you in. He doesn't flash a wad of money or open a box of chocolates to lure you. He simply is the gate. It's up to you whether to enter…or not.

It's a choice with an obvious upside. So why doesn't everyone dash through this gate?

For one thing, the gate is small. The road that leads to eternal life is narrow and only a few find it (Matthew 7:14).

As if that's not tough enough, Jesus says in Matthew 19:23-24 (NLT), "I tell you the truth…it is easier for a camel to go through the eye of a needle than for a rich person to enter the Kingdom of God!" So, does that mean multimillionaires and the ultra-powerful, super-wealthy Old Testament guys like Joseph and King David couldn't get into heaven? I don't think so. I think the kind of rich that keeps us from entering the kingdom of God refers to whatever baggage blocks us from entering the gate. It's whatever inflates self and ego and tricks us into viewing ourselves as bigger than God. We become so rich in self-importance and self-reliance that we don't see our need for Him. We fall for Satan's original pickup line to Eve: "You will be like God" (Genesis 3:5). And if we are like God we certainly don't need a savior like the pitiful, poor, wretched, blind, and naked of the world do.

Jesus is the gate. You've got to enter through Him to be saved. But you have to be small enough to fit. You have to be skinny enough to travel the narrow road. You have to let go of whatever baggage keeps you from fitting through the proverbial eye of the needle.

So, what does all this have to do with Big Sid?

Big Sid was a nothing—the Worst in Show. He was big in size, but small in every other way. He was a walking skeleton. He had nothing, owned nothing, was nothing. He didn't hesitate to enter Mark's car because he was a broken-down, worthless pile of skin and bones with absolutely nothing to lose.

Could this be the same way God wants us humans to spiritually enter the kingdom of heaven? Sometimes our egos and self-importance are too inflated to let us squeeze through that small gate. Our obsession with accumulating too many temporary worldly possessions makes us too wide to travel the narrow road. Basing our security and our identities on the size of our savings accounts, 401Ks, and stocks and bonds makes it impossible for us to pass through the eye of the needle.

Bottom line: We've got to be like Big Sid if we want to get into the kingdom of heaven. When Jesus opens the tailgate we must not hesitate to enter in and choose Life. But if you've got too much stuff and you can't let it go, you won't be able to fit in that wagon.

You say you just can't dump your fancy designer clothes and

shoes to live life in sackcloth and sandals? You don't have to. You just have to have an epiphany that will change your life. You just have to realize the truth of Revelation 3:17: "You say, 'I am rich; I have acquired wealth and do not need a thing.' But you do not realize that you are wretched, pitiful, poor, blind and naked."

We all need a spiritual reality check. We all need to open our eyes and see ourselves as God sees us—without all the external worldly trappings that cloak our true spiritual selves.

You and I may be more like Big Sid than we think.

Here I am! I stand at the door and knock. If anyone hears my voice and opens the door, I will come in and eat with that person, and they with me (Revelation 3:20).

Consider This:

Do you have baggage in your life that's making it hard for you to fit through the eye of the needle or walk the narrow road? What makes it tough for you to let it go? What might you gain of much greater worth if you released it? What choice will you make?

His Master's Keeper

Let God Protect You

His will is our hiding place.
CORRIE TEN BOOM

Sharon loves to fish. She doesn't mind fishing alone—that is, without other people—but she always takes Boomer, her 120-pound Great Pyrenees. Boomer is a great companion and protector.

One day Sharon and Boomer were fishing up high in the Kern River Canyon in Central California. This area is part of the Sequoia National Forest. Various types of wildlife may be found there, including coyotes, bears, cougars, and snakes.

Sharon was doing pretty well with her fishing, but Boomer seemed very nervous about their surroundings. Sharon ignored Boomer's concern at first, carefully climbing down the hill to fish closer to the water. That was when she heard strange sounds. She thought maybe she had better heed Boomer's cautionary behavior. She climbed back up the hill, Boomer sticking very close. Sharon figured they were out of harm's way so she stood on a bridge and dropped her line into the water once more. Boomer began acting even more nervous, and started trying to nudge her closer to her car. When she finally reeled up her line and started walking,

Boomer gently put his mouth on her wrist and pulled her to her vehicle.

Once they were on their way down the hill, Boomer relaxed and Sharon felt that maybe he had saved her from some serious harm. That night she heard that there was a cougar attack right where they had been fishing. Because Boomer had warned her of danger on other fishing trips, she knew she needed to pay attention when his nervousness persisted. She believes he would have fought and maybe given his life to save hers.

Boomer the dog was his master's keeper. My husband, Steve, is mine. He always tries to keep me safe. He did that yesterday when we took what I thought was a rather dangerous trip. Steve is a farmer and oversees many acres of land. He took me with him to a field where some farm work was being done way out in the middle of nowhere. There is a paved road for most of the way. But then, to get to the field, we had to drive on a road filled with very sticky mud.

I could see the danger in driving this road. It would have been impossible without a four-wheel-drive vehicle. This, of course, was what we had. Still, if I had been alone there was no way I would have even attempted it. But for Steve, it was old hat. He knew he could keep me safe and he thought it would be an adventure for me. So he just said, "Hold on, here we go!" Once we started, there was no stopping until the end. If we had stopped, we would have been horribly stuck in the heavy mud. I held on, prayed, screamed at times—and we both laughed, knowing Steve was a capable driver.

When we reached our destination, our truck was covered in mud. We could hardly see out the windows! Steve took care of his business and we visited with two other workers, George and Lupe, who laughed at me when I told them of our adventure. Then we took a less exciting route back to the main road and traveled thirty miles to our home. The danger I had sensed was real, but I had been safe in the hands of someone who knew how to handle such peril.

Many centuries ago, the Israelite prophet Elisha was in peril. The king of Israel was at war with the king of Aram. God had been giving Elisha intelligence about the Aramean army's movements that allowed Israel to keep foiling their efforts. When the king of Aram found out, he ordered his men to locate Elisha so he could capture the prophet. They discovered Elisha was in the city of Dothan.

A strong army was sent to Dothan. Elisha's servant woke up the next morning and saw these enemy forces surrounding the city. He was terrified at this danger. But Elisha knew that God was keeping him safe. He told his servant, "'Don't be afraid…Those who are with us are more than those who are with them.' And Elisha prayed, 'Open his eyes, LORD, so that he may see.' Then the LORD opened the servant's eyes, and he looked and saw the hills full of horses and chariots of fire all around Elisha" (2 Kings 6:16-17).

God delivered this huge army into Elisha's hands. Elisha persuaded Israel's king not to kill them. Instead, they feasted and were sent home to tell their king what had happened. His raids on Israel's territory stopped.

Boomer's job was to take care of Sharon, and he did it as well as a dog could. Steve loves me and does his best to keep me safe. But they aren't all-powerful like God is. No matter what dangers we may face, if we trust God and stick to His path, He will keep us safe in Him.

We do not want you to be uninformed, brothers and sisters, about the troubles we experienced in the province of Asia. We were under great pressure, far beyond

*our ability to endure, so that we despaired of life itself.
Indeed, we felt we had received the sentence of death.
But this happened that we might not rely on ourselves
but on God, who raises the dead. He has delivered us
from such a deadly peril, and he will deliver us again
(2 Corinthians 1:8-10).*

Consider This:

*Has a pet or human ever saved you from danger? What
happened? What did you learn? Has God ever kept you
from sliding down a dangerous path? How did this influ-
ence your faith?*

Part III

Tales to Light Your Path

Stuart

Gentledog Stuart
Care and Share

*Three keys to more abundant living: caring about
others, daring for others, sharing with others.*
WILLIAM ARTHUR WARD

S tuart is a kind, considerate Welsh corgi gentleman…er, gentledog. When he wants us to go out and play, he asks. He does this by standing in front of his desired human playmate. Okay, so sometimes he also barks very loudly and obnoxiously—which isn't the best of manners—but at least he's polite enough to state his request.

One of Stuart's favorite outdoor pursuits is playing ball. When the ball is thrown across the backyard, both Stuart and Squitchey, our much smaller terrier mix, take off after it in a huge rush. If Stuart gets there first he'll pick it up, but then allow Squitchey to take it from him and run it back to their human play partner. When they were younger, both dogs would have their mouths on the ball and run side by side. But now that Stuart is a little older and slower, he lets Squitchey do the legwork as he follows proudly behind her.

There is another way Stuart cares about and shares with Squitchey. When I put a dish on the floor for the dogs to lick, Stuart licks first as the alpha dog. But at times, he licks only one half of the plate. He leaves the other half untouched so Squitchey can have it. I have seen him do this repeatedly. Does Stuart know fractions? I don't know how he figures it out, but I think it's amazing! As a dog, does Stuart do this out of consideration, or is it just coincidence? Much as I'd like to think it's on purpose, I suspect the real answer is that God allows it to teach me a lesson.

I like to share, but in this life it's easy to get wrapped up in my own world and forget to care about others. My intentions are huge, but my actions are minute. For instance, when we moved into our new home five years ago, I had every intention of hosting a barbecue for our neighbors. When the neighbors on the north side of our house had a baby, I intended to give them a baby shower. We did visit both sets of neighbors and get to know them. But now they have both moved away and my good intentions never came to fruition. They got lost in the shuffle of time.

I've also wanted to share our apples. We have a beautiful apple tree in our backyard. These apples make wonderfully tart pies. They are a Fleishauer specialty. My intention is to make some of these apple pies for my new neighbors—or perhaps invite them over and enjoy the pies together. It will be a sacrificial gift that I will enjoy giving. When I bake the pies, I will thank God for the apples and think about how Stuart's sharing sets an example.

I appreciate what God has shown me about sharing through Stuart, but He has an even better story in the Old Testament book of 1 Kings. The prophet Elijah had declared that Israel would suffer a drought because of their idolatry (1 Kings 17:1). God then ordered Elijah into hiding. First he went to a wilderness area and was fed by ravens. Then God sent Elijah to the home of a widow in the town of Zarephath of Sidon who He had commanded to feed the prophet.

This widow was extremely poor. When Elijah asked her for bread, she told him she had just a small amount of flour and oil.

She said she was going to use them to make one last meal for her son and herself and then they would die. Elijah told her to do what she'd said, but first to make and bring him a small cake of bread. He promised if she did this, God would keep supplying her with oil and flour till the drought was over. She trusted God and obeyed Elijah. She shared her food, God kept His promise, and her flour jar and oil jug never ran out no matter how much she used.

Both Stuart and the widow were willing to care about others and not just themselves. That's what I want to do also. Stuart shared his plate, the widow shared her food, and through their examples, I want to share my apples.

Command them to do good, to be rich in good deeds, and to be generous and willing to share (1 Timothy 6:18).

Consider This:

What is the most special thing someone else has ever shared with you? How did it meet your needs or bless your life? Do you have something you could share to help others, or even just make them happy?

If the Dog Says "I Do"
Seek God's Guidance

If you can't pray a door open, don't pry it open.
LYELL RADER

Jody didn't usually go for May–December romances but Snoop was the sweetest, most charming guy she'd ever met in her life. She was in her mid-twenties and he was only six weeks old when they were introduced. It was love at first sight. Jody couldn't resist the charms of the boisterous and handsome golden retriever puppy and knew in her heart that he was the one. Snoop became her canine soul mate. She couldn't have been more blessed.

It was a completely different story with males of the *human* species.

Jody had met enough Mr. Wrongs to fill a baseball stadium and had been through several failed relationships. Mr. Right was proving harder to find than an ultra-rare Honus Wagner baseball card. There are 57 known Honus Wagner cards in the world, but Jody's universe seemed to have zero eligible men. By her account she'd gone on close to a million blind dates—or at least it felt that way to her.

When Number 999,999 opened the front gate to her walkway, Jody had a flicker of hope. He *looked* nice. But he'd have to pass the

Snoop test. Any potential suitor had to realize it wasn't only Jody he would be dating. It was a package deal: a girl and her dog. Jody let Snoop out and hung back on the porch to see what would happen. Snoop bounded down the steps, tail wagging, full of expectation…and the guy jumped back six feet before Snoop even had a chance to sniff him out. Jody shouted, "Oh, don't worry, he won't bite. The worst he'll do is lick you to death."

Number 999,999 recoiled as if she'd told him the dog had a combination of lice and leprosy. *Lick?* His tone of voice implied disgust to the nth degree.

Jody's flicker of hope went out. Number 999,999 would be the last straw. She swore she was done with dating and decided Snoop was all the man she needed.

Of course, a few days later her roommate set her up at a restaurant with Blind Date Number 1,000,000. The date with Rick exceeded Jody's expectations, but she didn't want to get her hopes up. She cut right to the chase and invited him home to meet her dog. It didn't matter if Rick was charming, handsome, and gainfully employed. If he and Snoop didn't hit it off—it was *three strikes you're out!*

Jody stood in the shadows of her elevated porch and watched as Rick's car pulled up in front of her vintage Craftsman-style house. As he opened the front gate, Snoop rushed down the steps and galloped straight toward yet another gentleman caller.

Jody fought to keep that tiny ember of hope alive in her heart. She'd never had a double win situation before. She and Snoop both had to be crazy about a guy who was crazy about them. Even if everything was perfect between her and Rick, and even if Rick liked Snoop, if Snoop didn't bond with Rick it was a deal-breaker.

Jody held her breath and prayed. Her romantic destiny was about to be decided by a dog.

Snoop came at Rick like a smiley-faced guided missile. Rick stood his ground and smiled back. Then, in a gesture that still warms the cockles of Jody's heart, Rick dropped down on all fours and met Snoop with a big embrace. They bonded like long-lost twins and wrestled all over the grass. As Rick let Snoop lavish his face with "disgusting" licks and kisses, Jody knew Rick was the one-in-a-million. Before he even walked through her front door, she knew the three of them would be a family.

Time proved those matchmaking instincts were right.

Jody and Rick made sure they got married in a grassy outdoor setting so Snoop could attend. When Rick whistled, Snoop the ring bearer, wearing a collar of flowers, padded down the aisle with the bands. Of course, a honeymoon fit for three had to be arranged—a month-long tour of the national parks. And when Rick went back to work at his RV repair shop, Snoop rode with him and had his own place at the shop to hang out.

A long time ago, in a land far away, someone else was faced with the challenge of finding the right mate. Abraham wanted his son Isaac to marry a girl from their homeland, not one of the local Canaanite bachelorettes. So, Abraham loaded ten camels with expensive gifts and sent his servant packing. The servant wasn't told who the special girl was, only that God would send an angel ahead to assist him. After a long journey, the servant brought his camels to the well just outside the town where Abraham's relatives lived. Here's his account of what happened next from Genesis 24:42-46 (NLT).

> When I came to the spring, I prayed this prayer: "O LORD, God of my master, Abraham, please give me success on this mission. See, I am standing here beside this spring. This is my request. When a young woman comes to draw water, I will say to her, 'Please give me a little drink of water from your jug.' If she says, 'Yes, have a drink, and I will draw water for your camels, too,' let her be the one you have selected to be the wife of my master's son."

Before I had finished praying in my heart, I saw Rebekah coming out with her water jug on her shoulder. She went down to the spring and drew water. So I said to her, "Please give me a drink." She quickly lowered her jug from her shoulder and said, "Yes, have a drink, and I will water your camels, too!"

Ta da! Wedding bells for Rebekah and Isaac, just like for Jody and Rick all those centuries later.

With matrimony and other matters we consider important, God has a variety of ways to inform our decisions. His toolbox includes His Word, His Spirit, wise parents, friends, and counselors, and even plain old common sense. But for some jobs, God occasionally uses signs as well. He gave Gideon a fleece, three wise men a star, and Abraham's servant a young woman's offer to water camels. So, why not use the instant bonding of a canine soul mate and prospective hubby to help point Jody to the man of her dreams?

Yes, sometimes God even has a dog or two in that toolbox of His.

The LORD will guide you always (Isaiah 58:11).

Consider This:

Do you seek God's guidance in your life? What are some ways He has informed your decisions? Did He ever give you a sign? How have His answers strengthened your faith? Is there someone you might encourage by sharing the uniquely personal way God has led you?

Skunk Wars
Learn and Live

Do not look where you fell, but where you slipped.
African Proverb

There's an old saying: "Live and learn." Annie the dog didn't get the memo—at least with respect to skunks. Thankfully, the results of her actions were more fragrant than fatal, but they still got her into lots of trouble.

Annie was my friend Martha's smart and sassy border collie/cocker spaniel mix. Martha believes that the first time Annie got skunked, she thought she was approaching a big, fluffy black and white cat. Annie wasn't pleased with the results. Ever after, she would go into hunter mode whenever she saw a skunk…and would inevitably get the worst of the encounter.

Way too often Annie went out in the yard to do her business, only to come in reeking from her failure to learn from past experiences. But perhaps her most intense skunk encounter happened on one never-to-be-forgotten Sunday morning.

Martha's house had a crawl space beneath it. Screens at different locations provided access. Martha had seen a gardener fiddling with one of them, and warned him to be sure it was properly secured in place. On this morning, Martha had let Annie into the yard and was making coffee. She heard muffled barking and went to retrieve her dog. But Annie was gone. Momentarily, Martha wondered if there was a hole in the fence. Then she turned and saw a screen off one of the crawl space openings. Oops!

Martha looked through into the crawl space. She couldn't see Annie, but she could hear her. Hurrying back inside, Martha went to the front bedroom. The muffled barking was clearer here, and she could smell skunk.

Martha rushed out her front door and pulled the screen off a second crawl space entrance. Annie had cornered a mama skunk and her babies. She would bark. They would spray. She would bark. They would spray. And on it went. Annie refused to see the black and white truth—she would not win this battle!

Martha started phoning for professional help, but wasn't finding anyone who'd come out. About that time she got a call from her employer. Martha was a producer for NBC News. They informed her she needed to be on a plane for Hawaii that night to work on a story.

In desperation, Martha phoned a friend who occasionally did some doggie day care for her. This friend knew Annie well. She was also more petite than Martha and could do what Martha couldn't—squeeze into that crawl space and drag Annie out.

Martha's friend managed to retrieve a dirt-covered, reeking Annie from under the house. Even as Annie was being dragged to the friend's car for cleanup and dog-sitting, she was straining at her leash to go back and keep giving those skunks "what-for." Annie never did live and learn with respect to skunks. She chased them every chance she got for the rest of her life.

Failure to learn from getting skunked is not confined to canines. A certain biblical character had this failing too—in Technicolor. Ahab was King of Israel in the time of the Divided Kingdom. He married an evil pagan Baal worshipper named Jezebel, and began to worship Baal himself. Scripture tells us that Ahab "did more to arouse the anger of the LORD, the God of Israel, than did all the kings of Israel before him" (1 Kings 16:33).

In judgment for his own and his kingdom's idolatry, God sent a drought proclaimed by the prophet Elijah. Three years later the drought ended in a contest between Elijah and—count 'em—450 prophets of Baal. It was a contest to see whose god would send down fire and consume an offering made on Mount Carmel. You could say that those prophets—and by extension, Ahab and Jezebel— got skunked. Their dry offering wasn't touched by fire, while Elijah's soaking wet sacrifice was totally consumed (1 Kings 18:22-39).

The point of that little exercise was to show Ahab and all Israel that God was God! Ahab didn't get the memo. He didn't turn from idolatry to God except very temporarily when he found himself in dire straits. Elijah, and God, gave him every chance not only to live and learn, but to learn and live by following the Lord. Sadly, he persisted in evil and kept getting "sprayed," not by a skunk, but by the results of his own reeking actions—which included complicity in murder—until he and his infamous queen met their divinely decreed deaths.

If truth be told, we all have areas where we can be like Annie and Ahab. We can fight what our Master is trying to show us. We can persist in attitudes and actions that are getting us skunked. Jesus squeezed into the crawl space of death to drag us out, reeking with sin, and cleanse us—but we still have our skunk-chasing old natures to deal with. Thankfully, we also have God's Spirit. He is calling us to follow Him in the sweet-smelling paths of righteousness. Will you learn and live?

For you were once darkness, but now you are light in the Lord. Live as children of light (for the fruit of the light consists in all goodness, righteousness and truth) and find out what pleases the Lord (Ephesians 5:8-10).

Consider This:

Are you fighting a losing battle with a skunk in your life? How are you getting sprayed? What support might you get from Scripture and other believers that would help you learn and live?

No Other Dogs Before Me
Some Things Can't Be Shared

God is indeed a jealous God—
He cannot bear to see
That we had rather not with Him
But with each other play.
EMILY DICKINSON

Chris is a busy guy. He's a physician who runs a department at a major Los Angeles hospital. He's also a part-time screenwriter. He works out regularly, enjoys an active social life, and travels. And he has a dog named Luna that he loves very much. Luna loves him back—unconditionally. But she sits home alone for long periods of time, pining because her master is a busy guy!

At one point Chris, a twenty-first century male, sensitive to the needs of the opposite sex, felt pangs of guilt over leaving his girl Luna by herself. Since quitting his job to be Luna's full-time companion was not an option, Chris decided to find Luna a four-legged friend.

Chris hit the animal shelter circuit with the determination of a recently single guy out on the prowl. It was exhausting. He had forgotten how difficult it was to find the right one. Too many dogs, too little time!

One day, a cute face caught Chris's eye. It belonged to a male half-Chihuahua, half-Something Else. Normally, Chris didn't go for Chihuahuas. But since this dog was a mix, maybe his reservations about the breed wouldn't apply.

The dog wagged his tail when Chris gave him the eye, then bounced around like a pinball when Chris approached. *Rambunctious* was the first word that came to Chris's mind. That could spell trouble—but it could also mean a fun, interesting, perky personality. So, after a few belly rubs and face licks, Chris impulsively decided that Comet was the Luna companion he'd been seeking.

As dog pals, Luna and Comet were fine. They kept each other company in the usual dog ways: romping, pouncing, and gnawing at each other. Luna seemed pleased to share her space with this new dog.

But she was *not* pleased to share her master.

When Chris came home, it would be an Olympic sprint to see who crossed the finish line to Chris first. If Comet got the jump on Luna and was first to greet Chris, Luna would bound up and muscle Comet out of the way. Once when Chris's mom came for a visit, Comet tried to climb into her lap. Luna dashed over and bit Comet's ear. Chris was appalled. He shook a disciplinary finger in Luna's face and shouted, "Bad dog!" In the heat of the moment, Luna bit Chris's hand and drew blood. Chris was shocked at this unheard-of act of violence and banished the offender into the backyard.

After Chris cooled down, he went outside and apologized to Luna. She was sorry too, licking Chris's hand and face. It was then that Chris realized he loved Luna but only liked Comet. He decided he had to give Comet up for adoption. Luna was a jealous dog and would have no other dogs before her. That's the way it was—and still is.

Chris put out the word, and amazingly, a nurse at work was looking for a small dog. Introductions were made. The nurse took

Comet home to her family of three young boys and their dad. To this day, the nurse tells Chris they absolutely love this dog. He sleeps with the boys and is utterly adored and worshipped.

Chris had the best intentions when he brought a dog home to be Luna's friend. But he discovered a trait in Luna he hadn't seen before—that she is a jealous dog. In her canine heart-of-hearts she could not tolerate sharing the intimate loving bond she had developed with Chris.

Jealousy isn't a trick Luna learned in school—it's a complex emotional response. Humans get jealous too, and so does God. And though the jealousy we and our dogs feel is not motivated by the pure, holy love that God's is, it can give us a tiny hint of what our Lord feels when we bring home other gods and place them on the altars of our hearts.

Check out Exodus 20:5 (NLT), "I, the LORD your God, am a jealous God who will not tolerate your affection for any other gods."

If God gave Luna the ability to speak, she'd tell Chris, "I, Luna your dog, am a jealous dog who will not tolerate your affection for any other dogs."

It's one thing to get nipped on the hand by a jealous mutt, but it's an entirely different matter to anger a jealous God. Take a look at Deuteronomy 6:15 (NLT), "For the LORD your God, who lives among you, is a jealous God. His anger will flare up against you, and he will wipe you from the face of the earth."

Wow! While God may not wipe us off the face of the earth the next time we arouse His jealousy, we must do our best not to make the Lord jealous. And the best way to do this? "Love the LORD your God with all your heart and with all your soul and with all your strength" (Deuteronomy 6:5).

God loved you first, with a love incredible beyond comprehension—so be very careful who or what you bring into your heart, the temple of the living God, the home of the Holy Spirit. Don't let it get soiled and diminished by other gods—not just for His sake, but for yours!

Do you not know that your bodies are temples of the Holy Spirit, who is in you, whom you have received from God? (1 Corinthians 6:19).

Consider This:

Is there anyone or anything that is first in your heart before God? How is this affecting your life? How do you think God feels about it? Considering God's pure and measureless love for you, are you willing to remove this idol and put God first again?

Spitfire Spit and Polished

Train Today, Gain Tomorrow

Life is the soul's nursery—
its training place for the destinies of eternity.
WILLIAM MAKEPEACE THACKERAY

Growing up the youngest of five children, there was always something going on. Getting a dog was one of the wonderful memories. We bought our little Boston terrier from a family that went to our church. We picked him out before he was ready to leave his mom, so the wait to get him seemed endless.

Finally, Dad and my brother Darrell went to pick him up. They brought home this tiny bundle of black and white fur. He had big, bulging black eyes and a black button marking on his forehead. Darrell gently put the puppy down on the floor as we all gathered around him. He couldn't have weighed more than a couple of pounds and all of it was shaking. Mom said, in her typical mom fashion, "Oh, poor little thing. Let's warm up some milk for him."

The next event was to name our new canine friend. After some common names were tossed out, Darrell shouted, "I know, I know! Spitfire!" He had just completed a Spitfire model airplane. A Spitfire was a little bomber plane that seemed to never give up. Darrell just knew this little guy would live up to the name. Everyone loved it, so the family puppy was Spitfire from that moment on.

Spitfire was a very smart little dog. We didn't care about teaching him tricks, but we needed to train him to live with his seven new humans. Spitfire was allowed in the backyard and den, but not in any other rooms. He was permitted to come into the house only through the back door. When he came to the front door he was told, "No Spitfire, you have to go to the back." Whoever said this would then run to the back door, open it, and call him. In just a few seconds, he would show up at the back door and contentedly walk in.

Spitfire had a little rug in front of the den television where he liked to snooze. But Mom's rule was that he had to sleep in the backyard at night. When it was time to let him out, one of us would walk up to him and he would start to snore loudly. He thought this would change our minds. But Mom was strict, and she always prevailed in the end.

Even though Spitfire knew what was expected of him, he sometimes had other ideas. One day, Darrell and Dad got on Dad's Honda 90 motorcycle and took off down the back alley. Spitfire was told to stay home, and they thought all the doors and gates were closed. But our little dog found a way to get out, and he ran behind them, barking all the way. Darrell turned around and ordered him home, but Spitfire didn't obey. Before they got to the end of the alley, Dad stopped the Honda and got off. He looked down at Spitfire and pointed toward the house. "Go home, Spitfire! Go home!"

Spitfire knew when Dad yelled, he had better listen. He turned around, hung his head, and slowly started walking home. Dad shouted, "Run home, Spitfire!" Spitfire rapidly picked up his pace. Dad and Darrell followed him so they could secure whatever opening he had escaped through. Then they jumped back on the Honda and took off again.

Apparently Spitfire had some sort of secret escape plan, because he got out of the backyard again. This time he ran in the opposite direction. He ended up at our pastor's home several blocks away. The pastor's family thought they recognized our little dog, so they called him over. Spitfire came and they played with him in their front yard. When everyone got tired they decided to ask him in for a cool drink of water. They all walked in the front door and invited Spitfire to come with them. Somehow Spitfire knew it was their front door. He walked up the front porch steps and stopped. They tried to coax him to come in, but he had been trained not to enter the front door, and he would not break this rule.

Someone in our pastor's family had heard about his training. They went to the back door and called him. Spitfire instantly ran to the back door, walked in, and sat down. They invited him into their living room, but it was near the front door, and he declined. They gave him water and called us to let us know they had him. The whole family was amazed at the level of training Spitfire had learned. The pastor was so impressed that he used Spitfire in his Sunday sermon on obedience.

When we got Spitfire home, Dad didn't know if he should yell at our dog for disobeying or praise him for his display of manners at the pastor's home. He decided on the latter. Spitfire's story traveled fast through our little town of Shafter. He was known as the polite little dog that understood how to follow directions.

Spitfire didn't ask for forgiveness in words, but that evening he sat close to my dad. It seemed to be a sign of affection and a request for forgiveness. Dad loved Spitfire and forgave him. His place in the family had not been altered. Our love for him had not diminished.

Like Spitfire, I knew what was expected of me, but sometimes chose to do otherwise. My dad taught me to drive on our farm when I was about ten. As I got older, he taught me the rules of the road. I had no problem getting my driver's license at 16. Mom and

Dad then let me drive to the grocery store alone. Right after getting that privilege, I was stopped by a policeman. I had been speeding as I crossed the railroad tracks.

I pulled over to the side of the road like the officer wanted me to. Then I saw my dad right behind him. I thought, "Hallelujah, I'm saved!" But to my horror, Dad just talked to the cop for a moment and then took off again in his pickup, leaving me to face my predicament on my own. The policeman just gave me a warning, and I was grateful. But I knew Dad had seen what happened. When I got home, he waited for me to come and talk to him about it. He listened calmly and patiently. He knew that I had gone through enough anguish with the law and didn't need more pain from him. He told me that if I'd gotten a ticket, I would have had to take care of it myself. No more was said.

My respect for Dad grew even more because of that incident. I realized his rules were meant for my good. I won't say I never sped again, but for the most part, my driving reflected his training.

Dad trained Spitfire and me for our gain. Our loving Heavenly Father also trains us for our good. He even gives us a timeless training manual called the Bible to guide us. Paul explains to Timothy in 2 Timothy 3:16-17, "All Scripture is God-breathed and is useful for teaching, rebuking, correcting and training in righteousness, so that the servant of God may be thoroughly equipped for every good work."

Spitfire walked through the door of Dad's training and gained a reputation as a well-mannered dog. Dad's training gained me greater safety on the road. If you submit to your earthly parents and the Lord, who knows what gain their training may bring you?

*I hold fast to your statutes, LORD; do not let me be put
to shame. I run in the path of your commands, for you
have broadened my understanding (Psalm 119:31-32).*

Consider This:

*What have you gained from your parents' training? From
God's training? In what areas are you tempted to run out
of God's gate? What consequences might this bring? What
would encourage you to run home to Him instead?*

Hook, Line, and Milk Jug
Look Before You Leap

*Look before you leap, for snakes
among sweet flowers do creep.*
PROVERB

Texene and her husband, Mac, were headed to the lake to go fishing for crappie. They had chosen two lucky dogs to go with them (out of eight eager candidates). Skipper the Lab, Mac's constant companion, got picked—as well as Whistle, their nutty two-year-old German shorthair pointer. While Skipper was a veteran fisherdog, this would be Whistle's first adventure on the water.

After an awkward spraddle-legged landing into the pontoon boat, Whistle quickly got his sea legs. As Mac took off, Whistle hopped on the seat next to Texene, who grabbed a captain's hat, turned it sideways, and put it on his head. Face into the wind, Whistle was the perfect picture of a canine sea captain.

Mac anchored the boat at their favorite spot and they dropped their minnow-hooked lines gently over the side. The dogs loved watching the bobbing corks and would bark each time a fish was landed. After pulling in a good haul, Mac headed to a shady spot for lunch. Whistle kicked back next to him, enjoying the breeze.

Suddenly, Whistle's ears perked up and his head cocked in high alert. He started spinning in his seat like a top. Something incredibly exciting in the water had caught his undivided attention. Without warning Whistle bailed over the side of the boat, swimming like his tail was on fire, focused like a laser beam on the object of his desire—a floating plastic milk jug.

Texene screamed, yelling for Whistle to come back! She wasn't worried about Whistle's ability to swim. She was scared about what lay under the surface of that milk jug. All she could think of was "that dreaded trot line." Trot lines are unattended fishing lines strung across the water with a series of baited hooks dangling down out of sight. They're usually tied between a couple of trees and milk jugs are attached as a warning to boaters.

Whistle continued to ignore Texene's calls. Her stomach churned with fear. Her mind played images of Whistle tangled up in those nasty hooks. As for Whistle, it was do or die. He was not about to be bested by some namby-pamby milk jug. With his jaws vise-gripped to the plastic handle, he swam until the line stretched to the breaking point, then snapped him back as if it were a bungee cord. Texene was afraid that if the hooks didn't snag Whistle first, her crazy dog would drown trying to fetch that milk jug.

As Mac maneuvered the boat alongside, Whistle gave a mighty tug and the trot line snapped. Texene sighed with relief as it drifted away. She and Mac grabbed Whistle and flopped him into the boat. He shook himself off, never letting go of his hard-won prize. He bounced all over the boat, wanting to play with that jug, and clueless how close he had come to being hooked into a worst-case scenario.

All Whistle knew was that he loved milk jugs. He had played with those cheap and plentiful toys ever since he was a puppy. He just didn't know what Texene knew—that the jug floating on the lake was attached to a very dangerous set of hooks hidden from sight. After Whistle leaped before he looked, he still had a choice.

He could've listened to Texene and come back to the safety of the boat. But instead he let his desires short-circuit his connection to his master as he swam headfirst toward danger.

We can take a holier-than-thou stance about how a dumb dog risked his life for a milk jug. But how often do we beings of higher intelligence leap before we look and get hooked going after milk jugs of our own design?

This happened to no less a man of God than the biblical King David. He was out for a leisurely nighttime stroll when he spied something that focused his eyes like a laser beam and caused him to throw caution to the wind: a gorgeous woman taking a bath.

God must have been shouting in His still, small voice, "No, David! Come back!" But David didn't listen. He only saw what was above the water's surface—a beautiful woman. He kept swimming toward the object of his desire, oblivious of the hooks that lurked below the bath water…like the fact that Bathsheba was married to another man.

David loved beautiful women—just like Whistle loved milk jugs. And just like Whistle, David ignored his Master and got snagged. He dragged Bathsheba into an affair, and she got pregnant. Hooked and re-hooked, David was pulled down deeper and deeper into the murky depths of sin. He sank as low as having Bathsheba's husband killed to cover up his guilt. But none of this was hidden from God's sight. God sent the prophet Nathan to confront David with his wrongdoing and proclaim the grave consequences of David being hooked by his lust and desire.

Nathan told David, "This is what the LORD says: 'Out of your own household I am going to bring calamity on you. Before your very eyes I will take your wives and give them to one who is close to you, and he will sleep with your wives in broad daylight. You did it in secret, but I will do this thing in broad daylight before all Israel'" (2 Samuel 12:11-12).

As if that wasn't rough enough, Nathan had more bad news for David: "Because by doing this you have shown utter contempt for the LORD, the son born to you will die" (2 Samuel 12:14).

All this calamity came upon David because he obeyed his passions instead of his Master. David knew adultery, lying, and murder were wrong. But he cast off all caution because he wanted that alluring lady as badly as Whistle wanted that milk jug. Texene knew about the hooks beneath the surface—and so did God.

Truth be told, we all have things that tempt us to leap before we look—things we lust for so much we don't care what lies beneath the surface. We all have things that make us deaf and blind to God's Word.

Before you jump out of the boat or veer off the path of righteousness to pursue the object of your desire, wait and check with your Master first. Look in the Word. Pray. Meditate. Listen to His still small voice calling to you.

Whatever your plastic milk jug is—love of money, sex, drugs, that brand new BMW, or even a box of chocolates—look to God before you leap!

My eyes are ever on the LORD, for only he will release my feet from the snare (Psalm 25:15).

Consider This:

What are the milk jugs in your life that tempt you to leap before you look? Have you ever gotten hooked? What were the consequences? Did God deliver you? What did you learn? What would you do differently as a result?

The Making of a Champion
Mentors Matter

*Mentor: Someone whose hind-
sight can become your foresight.*

ANONYMOUS

Chris has always loved basset hounds. She usually has two at any given time. Amos is her most recent canine family member. We all had fun getting to know him as a puppy. He made everyone laugh because he was so clumsy. When he walked around the house, he would knock things over. When he jumped on someone's lap (which wasn't acceptable behavior), he'd nearly topple the human. But he was so lovable and charming, everyone forgave him.

Amos is also a beautiful basset. Linda, his breeder, wanted to exhibit him at dog shows. When Chris told us, we couldn't help but laugh. Amos in the ring?

Linda didn't really think Amos would have much chance of winning, because his conformation took a little longer to mature. But she wanted to try. Linda would show him, but Chris would be involved in his training and be there to love, support, and care for him.

Chris took Amos to American Kennel Club handling classes

so he would know what was expected of him. He had to ride in a crate and stay in the crate for long periods of time. He had to learn not to be distracted by all the other people and dogs. He had to let strangers open his mouth and check his teeth. He had to let them run their hands over all parts of his body. He had to stay stacked, which means standing motionless while maintaining the proper basset hound pose. He had to be happy in the ring. These are all things we thought would be impossible for Amos because of his rambunctious behavior.

Basset hounds are shown on a low table. They walk up a ramp to get there. The first time Amos came to one, he walked around the back of the table and jumped on top. Another time, he was walking up the ramp and fell off. This didn't bother Amos. He just got back on and kept performing.

Amos also had to learn to be groomed. Bassets shed all year long, so they need a lot of brushing to get rid of this dead coat. Bassets' coats also tend to get stinky and oily, so they require frequent bathing. It's such a joy to get a 60-pound dog into the bathtub! Bassets also have toenails like bear claws. They need to be clipped short for the feet to look good. Since he was a little puppy, Amos has had his nails ground down with an instrument called a Dremel grinder. He has had to learn to tolerate this too—and he has!

Amos seems to know when he is going to a show. It's as if he has a sixth sense about this. He has learned how to behave in a hotel. He has learned to ride in an elevator without slinging slobber all over his human fellow passengers. He loves all the attention he gets. But Chris says it hasn't changed him—he's still the same goofball he always was. Show dogs like to do the same things other dogs do!

Last March, Amos was in his first show. After several more shows, he became a champion in July. His official title is Champion SoLow Craigwood's Amos.

No one who knew Amos dreamed that he could be trained to

compete, but Amos seems to love the ring. It was even more incredible to see him become a champion in such a short amount of time. But his breeder worked with him to bring him to his best, and his dog mom loved him, took care of him, and cheered him on. With all this mentoring and encouragement, I think maybe it never occurred to Amos that he wasn't a champion—so he became one!

Mentoring mattered for Amos the dog. It's crucial for people too. A teenage friend of mine has an incredible talent for making films. Ellen, along with her team, entered the Christian Youth Film Festival of Kern County in 2010. They took first place in almost every category.

Everyone on the team worked hard to do their very best, but the project became a huge part of Ellen. She wrote the film with others, but kept polishing it on her own until it was ready to shoot. She asked adults for advice on all aspects of making the film. She got lots of support from her parents, family, friends, and her film-making team—but she also always gave God the glory.

When it was time to submit the film, I remember how nervous she was, hoping it would make it to the finals and be shown at the Majestic Fox Theater. That evening, she and her team would barely get back in their seats from receiving an award when their names were called again. Every time, Ellen thanked the Lord. That night, with the support and mentoring of so many who loved her, Ellen was a champion—just like Amos!

Amos and Ellen had great potential, but they needed mentoring to grow and flourish. The same was true of a biblical character named Samuel. His mother had dedicated him to God before his birth. When he was still a very young boy, she brought him to serve in God's temple under Eli, the current high priest. But Samuel did not yet know God personally.

One night Samuel was sleeping and he heard someone calling him (1 Samuel 3). He assumed it was Eli and went to him. But

Eli said he hadn't called for the boy. When Samuel lay down, he heard the voice again. Once again, Eli denied he had called. But when it happened a third time, Eli realized God was calling Samuel. He told Samuel how to respond. God then gave Samuel his first prophecy—a judgment against Eli and his family. When Samuel was afraid to tell Eli, the old priest urged Samuel to reveal it and not hide anything. Though the Bible tells us Eli had his failings, he mentored Samuel well in this instance. God continued to be with Samuel and he grew up to be one of Israel's great prophets.

I believe God gave each of us special gifts and abilities. But to develop them, we need mentoring from Him and others. If we are willing to be mentored, and to mentor in return, we can all be champions for Him!

As Jesus was walking beside the Sea of Galilee, he saw two brothers, Simon called Peter and his brother Andrew. They were casting a net into the lake, for they were fishermen. "Come, follow me," Jesus said, "and I will send you out to fish for people." At once they left their nets and followed him (Matthew 4:18-20).

Consider This:

Have you had special people in your life to mentor you and help you grow? How did they encourage and guide you? What impact did it have? Who might you encourage and mentor to become a champion?

Playpen Theology
God Wants Our Hearts

*There can only be two basic loves...the love of
God unto the forgetfulness of self, or the love of
self unto the forgetfulness and denial of God.*

St. Augustine

My new puppy is proof that you can't judge the strength of a
dog's will by its size. Marley is tiny, but his resolve is huge. He is
also just clever enough to get his way despite my best efforts...at
least until I find him out!

That's just what happened with Marley's playpen. I got it so he
would have a protected place to play. He would be safely contained
inside, but have more room to romp around than if I crated him
when I couldn't watch him. I found a great model that could be
folded up and put in a carrying bag. It was lightweight and had a
zip-on top. This top and the pen's sides were mesh, so Marley could
get plenty of ventilation and enjoy looking at the outside world.
The playpen's floor also seemed ideal. It was made of a washable
material and was secured in place at various points with Velcro. I
loved that it could be removed for cleaning.

I didn't realize it could be removed for other purposes as well...
and not just by a human.

One evening shortly after setting up this new puppy play area in my office, I decided to leave Marley in his pen while I got dinner. When I returned, he was loose in the room. I was stunned. At first, I wondered if I'd simply forgotten to contain him. But I soon realized what had happened. Marley had tugged at the pen's floor, pulled it partway off its Velcro fasteners, and wriggled under the lightweight frame to escape.

In the days that followed, I tried sticking that floor piece down more firmly, but he kept pulling it up and getting out. I think he knew I didn't care for his Houdini antics. He didn't break out when I was watching. But every time I was gone for a while, my little Marley did it his way.

Finally, I had an idea. I flipped the playpen upside down so the zippered-on top was his new floor. I laid the old floor piece over the mesh for extra padding. Marley could no longer escape. Victory was mine—or was it?

Marley's little body had been captured. His heart was a different matter. He kept pawing at the old floor piece, flipping it back. He got up on his little hind legs and chewed at the pen's upper rim. Clearly, Marley's heart remained outside the playpen even if his body couldn't get there.

Like my dog, I've also had times when my heart was outside the playpen. One such period followed my father's death. I was an only child, and I feared my mother would latch on to me too tightly now that her husband of forty years was gone. I was young, single, and selfish. I was also guilt-ridden that I hadn't spent more time with Dad in his last months on this earth. Being with Mom and seeing her pain was like twisting a knife in that guilt wound. For all those reasons, I chafed at being in my mother's company and home.

All these years later, I'm ashamed of how I acted then. I spent as little time at Mom's house as I could. Finally, on one visit, I came down with some sort of inner ear problem and got vertigo. It was nothing serious, but I couldn't leave when I had planned. I had to wait till the problem subsided and I could safely drive the 90 miles back to my LA home.

In playpen theology terms, I believe God was trying to contain me for my good, and Mom's. I considered being with Mom a playpen I wanted to flee. I thought it might curtail my freedom, just as Marley felt his playpen did all those decades later. God, however, was trying to place me in a very different playpen—for Mom's good and my blessing. That playpen was the fifth of God's Ten Commandments: "Honor your father and your mother, so that you may live long in the land the LORD your God is giving you" (Exodus 20:12).

By avoiding spending time with Mom, I had been refusing to stay in that playpen. Finally, God flipped it upside down. I was forced to remain with her an extra day or two. I did not respond well. I pawed at the flooring and chewed at the pen's rim by expressing my frustration. Mom was rightfully hurt that I was so eager to leave. Rather than surrender my heart to the Lord and minister to the mother who needed me so badly, all I wanted to do was escape.

Mom was grieved, but she couldn't force my heart into the playpen any more than I could force Marley's. God could—but He chose to give us free will. Thankfully, He kept working on my heart. In later years, Mom and I drew much closer. But at the time, she took no joy in my extended visit with her, because she knew I didn't want to be there.

What Mom desired was for me to freely give my heart to her. That is also what God wants from us. Our Creator who made us knows that forced love isn't love at all. That's why we must choose to receive Him and embrace the playpens He has given us to protect and bless us. Jesus said, "Whoever has my commands and keeps them is the one who loves me" (John 14:21). God's commands are spiritual playpens meant to keep us safe from harm and accomplish His kingdom purposes. But simply going through the motions isn't enough. We must enter in willingly and love Him with our whole being.

I wrote the first draft of this story many weeks ago. As I sit tweaking it, Marley is playing on the floor. I've had him five months, and as he grows in his trust and love for me, he wants more and more to please me.

Over time, my trust and love for God have grown too. I've seen how His desires for me are for my good. And I've realized there is no better place to be than joyfully, willingly dwelling in the playpen of His loving care.

*And now, Israel, what does the L*ORD *your God ask of you but to fear the L*ORD *your God, to walk in obedience to him, to love him, to serve the L*ORD *your God with all your heart and with all your soul, and to observe the L*ORD'*s commands and decrees that I am giving you today for your own good? (Deuteronomy 10:12-13).*

Consider This:

When was your heart last outside the playpen with respect to God? What did you do? What was the result? Has your heart returned to the playpen? If not, why not? If so, what difference has it made?

Vengeance Is Mine, Sayeth the Dog

Let God Repay

Revenge, at first though sweet,
Bitter ere long back on itself recoils.
John Milton

When Keith was nine there were two things he treasured above all else. The first was his precious German shepherd/terrier mix named Fred. He was the dog every little boy dreams of—the perfect companion for long summer days, who never complained about getting dirty, who worshipped the very ground his boy walked on. And Keith loved Fred with all his heart.

The second thing Keith treasured above all other material things was the best Christmas gift he ever got from his parents: a 1/32 die-cast model of the coolest car on earth. James Bond's silver Aston Martin DB5, as featured in the film *Goldfinger*.

Manufactured by Corgi (not the dog), this imported precision machine was not to be confused with the domestic-made clunkier version of the Bond car. No, Keith's DB5 was not your common everyday toy car, but a work of art. To call this James Bond iconic miniature a toy car would be something just short of slander. This DB5 was a daydream come true for boys of Keith's generation. It was a kind of time machine that could transport a nine-year-old into the coolest, most suave and sophisticated adulthood, racing his DB5 through exotic foreign locales, beautiful assistant at his side, fighting evil super-spies with the latest incredible high-tech weapons.

Keith's DB5 may have been small enough to fit in his hand but it still had all the gadgets that made the Bond car so super cool. It had the extendable tire-slasher knock-off hubcaps. The bullet-proof shield that popped up from the trunk. Automatic rotating license plate. And best of all, his Bond car even had the ejector passenger seat to send the tiny bad guy holding a gun on Keith sailing up, out, and away.

Fred, on the other hand, did not have an elite Aston Martin pedigree. He was just your average domestic mutt. Four legs, a tail, two brown eyes—no special high-tech features. No X-ray vision or Cheetah-fast bionic legs or the ability to hula hoop. If Fred were a car, he'd be a family minivan.

But what Fred lacked in coolness or exoticism he made up for with qualities money can't buy. Keith told me Fred was the most loyal, loving, and energetic dog in the world—everything a nine-year-old boy could want!

There was a boy who lived around the corner from Keith who would occasionally drop over. Mario wasn't best friend material, but he was a convenient kid to have around when Keith needed a human playmate. He and Keith would play with the usual action figures and board games or romp around the backyard with Fred.

But what really put the twinkle in Mario's eyes was nothing less than Keith's Aston Martin DB5. Somehow, no matter what they were doing, Mario always found a way to get himself into the driver's seat of Keith's sports car and drive away on his own fantasy adventures.

One day, Keith felt the usual urge to be James Bond and went to get his car. It wasn't on the shelf where it was supposed to be. Keith tore his room apart trying to find his silver Aston Martin. He searched the whole house, then the entire yard to the point of exhaustion. He finally realized the horrific truth. His precious car was gone!

Looking back, Keith still recalls his profound feelings of loss and violation, probably the same he'd feel if his present adult car were stolen. Actually, after a moment of reflection, Keith said he felt worse about the $\frac{1}{32}$ scale Aston Martin.

Even as a kid, Keith didn't have to be Sherlock Holmes to come up with his number one suspect. When Keith went by Mario's house to inquire about his car, Mario's big sister told Keith that Mario was busy. Mario never confessed to the crime. But before the DB5 incident, Mario was always dropping by unannounced to play. Afterwards, he never came over again. Keith had no proof that Mario was the culprit and short of turning his house inside out, Keith would have to take Mario at his word: he was innocent. He didn't take the DB5. (Perhaps it was beamed up by aliens, or the victim of spontaneous combustion?)

Keith was devastated. But at least he still had his trusty pal, Fred, to lick his face and console him. Fred just listened as Keith ranted and spilled out his feelings about the stolen car.

Shortly after the car went missing, Mario and his brother were playing Frisbee in front of Keith's house. An errant toss sent the Frisbee flying over the fence and into Keith's backyard (Fred's domain). Mario had gone over to Keith's yard many times, and had no fear of gentle Fred, so he let himself in the gate to fetch his Frisbee.

Without warning, Fred attacked Mario and bit his hand. While not life-threatening, it was serious enough to send a crying Mario to the local hospital for stitches.

Later that night, Keith had a powwow with Fred. They locked eyes and silently communicated as boys and their dogs have done since the beginning of time. Without a word being spoken, Keith understood that Fred knew. His trusty dog companion knew Mario had been a very bad boy and took it upon himself to punish the thief. Up to that time, Fred had never laid a tooth on Mario. To this day, Keith truly feels Fred exacted the punishment on Mario that Keith could not. Even as a nine-year-old, Keith felt there was justice in the world.

How many of us have been wronged and there was nothing we could do about it? We didn't want to stoop to the level of the perpetrators, we had no proof, or whoever did us wrong was far bigger and stronger than us. But if we do nothing but dwell on thoughts and fantasies of revenge, it can eat us up inside. Negative thinking can take up large amounts of space in our minds, turning our countenances dark and angry, building up unhealthy amounts of poisonous unforgiveness and hate.

But it's not fair!

A building contractor recently swindled my wife and me out of a large sum of money. I hear it happens so much there's actually a television reality program in development called *Contractors from Hell.* I called the police to arrest the man, but they said it was a civil matter. We sued him and won, but discovered that collecting the money is a whole other ballgame. A collection agency charges 40 to 50 percent if they're successful in recovering any funds. Well-meaning friends told us to hire a hit man…or at least sic a "hit dog" like Fred on him.

Thinking about the wrong done to us churned up my insides. I couldn't sleep at night. I could relate to how angry and frustrated Keith felt about being ripped off by someone he trusted. And how in the world could we finish the house without recovering the missing money?

It would be so nice if God sanctioned a Revenge Day where you could inflict Old Testament punishment on your enemies without fear of reprisal. But like Warren G. Harding's birthday ever becoming a national holiday, Revenge Day ain't gonna happen.

Little Keith had Fred to look out for him. My wife and I came to realize we have Someone, too, who looks out for us. We had to let go of our feelings of violation, anger, and pain—and wait on God. We had to believe we were God's children and that He would take care of us like the best Father in the universe.

Just as nine-year-old Keith believed that Fred knew what Mario did and exacted justice—just as Keith could feel the burden of revenge lifted off his shoulders by Fred's intervention—so we must believe what God our Father says in Romans 12:19 (NASB): "Never take your own revenge, beloved, but leave room for the wrath of God, for it is written, 'Vengeance is mine, I will repay,' says the Lord."

This is gospel truth. God says never take your own revenge. He's the perfect Father who will take care of it for you.

Fred went to bat for Keith by biting Mario's hand. God has cared for my wife and me in a different way. He has lifted the hatred and need for revenge from my heart. He's gifted us with money to finish the house in ways that rival catching a fish with a coin in its mouth. Each time we receive this kind of monetary blessing, a little bell rings in my heart to remind me it's from God. I no longer daydream about ways to poison our contractor from hell. God has lifted that burden off me. Nowadays, I've been praying for the guy who cheated us to repent and be saved.

Fred loved Keith.

God loves us.

It's nice to have Someone looking out for your best interests.

The LORD works righteousness and justice for all the oppressed (Psalm 103:6).

Consider This:

Has someone ever wronged you and seemingly gotten away with it? How did it make you feel? Were you able to commit it to the Lord? How have you seen Him work in the situation? Have you forgiven the person or persons involved?

To Stray or Not to Stray
Stay Home with God

No man can follow Christ and go astray.
WILLIAM H.P. FAUNCE

The John Fleishauer family includes John, his wife, Sari, his daughter, Sierra, and two schnauzers. The dogs are nearly the same age and are both considered miniatures, even though they are somewhat different in size. Hangover is a gorgeous 23-pound male with a beautiful coat. He is tall and lean and stands like a champion, although in his heart he's still a warm, sweet little puppy. Sadie is smaller, at just ten pounds, and has a more hyper personality. She loves to jump from lap to lap until she decides which one to snuggle into for some nap time.

One day, after the family had left for work and school, Sadie got out of the yard through a loose fence board. This was her first time to escape. Hangover was too big to follow, so she was on her own. Sadie's family doesn't know how long she was out. It was a half-day at the school where Sari taught, so she came home early. Their home is in a quiet neighborhood, but it's near a very busy street. As Sari approached, she saw a little dog barking with all it had at a windmill on their neighbor's lawn. Her heart nearly jumped out of her chest when she realized that the silly dog was her Sadie. She opened the car door and yelled for Sadie to come. Sadie stopped barking instantly, gave Sari a huge puppy smile, pranced over to the car, and jumped in. She began kissing Sari the only way she knows how—all tongue.

When Sari got Sadie home, she carried the dog inside and they both sat on the couch while Sari caught her breath. She could tell Sadie knew she was in trouble by the way she had her ears pinned back. But the little dog continued her sweet puppy smile, apparently hoping that Sari would forget what had just happened. Sari figured it was in a dog's nature to roam and wasn't about to punish Sadie after the fact. John fixed the fence, and he and his family planted a garden where the loose board had been.

Leaving the yard was disobedient and foolish, but thanks to Sari, Sadie was protected from venturing further and reaching the busy street. Years ago, back in my "puppy days," I was foolish this way too. I disobeyed and wandered away, and I nearly got into big trouble.

I was 18 and had gone with some other young people on a missionary trip to Japan. We spent some time at a camp in the hills near Osaka. On our last day, we were told that a young woman had been stabbed near the camp the night before. We were warned not to leave the camp or go anywhere else alone.

But that evening, I felt sad to leave the people. I didn't feel like singing or celebrating. In spite of what we'd been told, I walked out of the camp alone and down the road next to a cliff which led to a river. I sat down and dangled my feet over the cliff's edge. Suddenly, I heard someone walking toward me. My imagination ran wild. I feared it was the stabber, out looking for another woman. Here I was, all alone in the dark. I was terrified. I stayed frozen until the person walked away. Then I begged the Lord to lead me back to safety. He did. I made it back to camp, and no one ever knew what I had done. But without God's leading and protection, I can only imagine what harm might have befallen me.

Sadie and I were both protected by someone wiser than ourselves who loved us. Our straying could have led to far worse consequences. Sadie could easily have been stolen or hit by a car. I could easily have been killed. The stabbing near camp was only one in a number of murders, suggesting the culprit may have been a serial killer. I was sitting alone on a tall cliff with a river below. He could have easily slain me that dark night and pushed me over the edge, and no one would have seen him.

The Bible talks a lot about sheep and how they go astray. Yesterday I drove by a small flock of sheep that live in my rural neighborhood. I watched what appeared to be a mother sheep nudging her lamb back into the flock from where it had roamed. She shoved her little lamb with her nose as he reluctantly joined the rest. It made me think of the parable of the lost sheep in the Bible (Luke 15:1-7). It tells about how a shepherd left the rest of his flock to find one lamb that was missing. That was always my favorite story growing up. I think I related to that lamb wanting to wander. I'm sure it was just out for adventure, like Sadie the schnauzer years later. Though I wasn't out for adventure that long-ago night in Japan, I strayed too far and could have paid an awful price. But my Good Shepherd stayed with me, watched over me, and brought me safely home.

The Bible tells us not to be foolish. We don't need to be like silly sheep. We can forsake our straying ways, draw near to our Good Shepherd, and stay safe in His loving care.

I am the good shepherd. The good shepherd lays down his life for the sheep (John 10:11).

Consider This:

Have you ever strayed from God? What were the results? How has the Lord been a Good Shepherd to you? In what ways might you need to come home to Him?

Squirrels and Girls
Beware of Life's Temptations

Opportunity may knock only once,
but temptation leans on the doorbell.
ANONYMOUS

When Erin was 13 she went on a family camping trip to Sleeping Bear Dunes in Michigan. They had a great time, as usual. Leaving the campground, Mom and Dad sat in front while Erin and her brother rode in back along with Gracie, their very independent and spirited golden retriever/Australian shepherd mix.

Being a warm day, Erin's brother rolled down the window so Gracie could stick her head out for some fresh air. There are few things in a dog's life more pleasurable than poking its head out of a moving car. Have you ever seen a dog do this without wearing a huge goofy grin on its face?

However, in a moment, Erin and her family were about to discover one of the few things Gracie found even more pleasurable than sticking her head out the window of a moving car—chasing squirrels!

Gracie jumped out the window.

Erin and her brother were in shock. One moment the dog

was in the car, and the next moment she was gone! Her brother instinctively held onto the leash as Gracie suddenly found something more pressing than chasing the squirrel—running for her life alongside the car to avoid being dragged or choked to death.

Dad heard the kids screaming from the backseat. Then he saw the family dog doing 25 miles per hour outside the car. He put two and two together and slammed on the brakes. The family piled out and retrieved a traumatized Gracie. There was no physical damage, just a very freaked-out dog.

Needless to say, for the rest of the ride home Erin and her brother kept the window rolled up so only Gracie's nose could poke out.

Dumb dog, huh?

But how many of us smart humans have ever "jumped out the window" before we looked? What's your squirrel? What's that all-encompassing obsession that makes you do dangerous, dimwitted, and downright stupid things?

For many of us guys, both single and not-so-single, it's girls. It's nothing new. It's been that way since the beginning of time. Literally.

God personally warned Adam not to eat of the forbidden fruit, but Adam leapt out the window and bit in as it was offered to him by Eve. As a consequence, childbirth would become an absolute bear for the ladies and men would have their share of pain working to put food on the table. And if that wasn't bad enough, now we all have to die.

Samson had a history of using prostitutes and fell in love with Delilah, a woman of questionable character. She was paid 1,100 shekels of silver by the Philistines to uncover the secret of Samson's super strength. Even though he knew that divulging the source of his power would have disastrous results, Samson leapt out the window and told Delilah about his long hair. As a consequence he got a bad haircut, was imprisoned, and had his eyes gouged out. Ouch.

A whole laundry list of Israel's kings took pagan wives and allowed those wives to lure them away from God and into idolatry.

And you'd think by now men would've learned from their mistakes. You'd think they would've realized that when you're zipping down the autobahn of life and spy a woman (not your wife) by the side of the road, it's not a good idea to jump out the window. But how many modern-day politicians, sports heroes, movie stars, and even priests and pastors have thrown caution to the wind and leaped out the window to chase a fleeting affair—only to do serious long-term damage to their careers and families?

And let's not let women and happily married men off the hook. Temptation isn't limited to chasing squirrels and girls. Its victims aren't limited to dogs and the high and mighty. Giving in to temptation is a national pastime. Shopping for things we want and don't need, constantly pursuing endless sales, specials, and the buy-one-get-one-frees of life…it's all the dark side of the American Dream. Your squirrel could be whatever makes you leap before you look. It's whatever pleasure you pursue that disregards God's Word.

To put it in old-fashioned Christianese: it's whatever causes you to sin.

It might be the usual suspects: sex, drugs, and rock 'n' roll. Or it could be that job that pays more—but compromises your morals. Or that new car or upscale home that beckons to you outside the window. They'd make you feel so much bigger, so much cooler—but would also slap you with serious debt and burden your family. It could be an addiction to food that makes you leap…into a quagmire of clogged arteries and heart disease. Even the pursuit of religiosity over a relationship with God can make you stumble, luring you into thinking you can get to heaven through works, not faith.

Fortunately, when we do leap out of moving vehicles, when we veer off the path of righteousness to pursue our lusts and passions, we have a loyal God who says He'll never leave us or forsake us. As children of God, no matter how far we stray, our Lord always has a tight grip on our leash. We may fall from grace, smack against the pavement, and be shaken up, but if we humble ourselves and confess our sins, God promises to forgive us and take us back into the car. Amen!

Watch and pray so that you will not fall into temptation. The spirit is willing, but the flesh is weak (Matthew 26:41).

Consider This:

Have you ever been tempted to "jump out the window" to chase a squirrel? What about it was irresistible, that lured you? What were the consequences? What did you learn? What do you find most helpful in resisting the squirrels that tempt you now?

Don't Pick at It or It Won't Get Well

Receive God's Forgiveness

Forgiveness is the answer to the child's dream of a
miracle by which what is broken is made whole
again, what is soiled is made clean again.

DAG HAMMARSKJÖLD

I had a treasured older friend who used to say, "Don't pick at it or it won't get well." My little rescue dog, Munchie, was living proof. When I started fostering him, he had some serious skin issues. There were "hot spots" on various parts of his body. He had been partially shaved so these sores could be exposed and treated. But despite the medication, they were still bothering him so much that he was constantly trying to lick his wounds. This, of course, just made matters worse and didn't let healing take place, so his rescue group gave me a cone. It was a plastic contraption shaped something like a megaphone and fit over his head. Theoretically, when this cone was tied in place it would keep the little guy from gnawing at his owies.

I soon discovered this particular cone didn't quite stop Munchie from picking at his wounds. Nor was his current medicine keeping them calmed down. I did some makeshift bandaging to get us through the night and scooted him off to my own vet the very next day.

Munchie's new doctor promptly recommended a slightly different medication and a new, larger cone. In short order, Munchie started feeling much better. He still wanted to lick at himself, but thankfully the new cone didn't let him. It was cumbersome and I wished I could remove it sooner, but I realized he had to wear it so his wounds would heal. It took time, but gradually the sores got better.

Munchie's healing wasn't a straight shot. There were a couple of minor flare-ups. I had to cone him again, though briefly. My vet also helped identify the source of his trouble. He determined that Munchie was severely allergic to fleas. Even one fleabite could cause a significant problem. He urged that I take precautions to keep all the four-foots in my household flea-free. My dogs are now on a once-a-month pill, and my kitties get a monthly topical application. These procedures have done the trick. I have now adopted Munchie and he is a healthy, happy dog.

Skin sores aren't the only wounds that may keep festering when licked. This same truth applies to emotional "owies" as well. I found this out firsthand with respect to a horribly painful hot spot of guilt involving my mother.

Mom was battling chronic leukemia for the last few years of her life. She had other health issues as well. At one point she was dealing with pneumonia, and had been hospitalized. When she came home, she still wasn't feeling right. A caregiver and I thought it might be due to anxiety and her weakened physical state. I reassured her over the phone and got feedback that she seemed to be doing better.

I wasn't quite at peace, though. A thought niggled at my brain.

Could she be having heart problems? But Mom preferred alternative therapies to Western medicine and fought going to more traditional doctors. Would she even be willing to see a cardiologist, and undergo testing?

It crossed my mind to call Mom's primary care physician and tell her what Mom's symptoms were. But I was in the midst of finishing a book manuscript. Mom had just been in the hospital, right? She was doing a bit better, wasn't she? And she had nurses at home. I pushed the thought aside and let things be.

A few days later, I spoke with Mom on a Sunday afternoon. She sounded upbeat and strong. I hung up and plowed into my manuscript work. Two hours later, a phone call shattered my calm. Mom had been rushed to the hospital. It turned out she'd had a life-threatening heart attack.

Munchie had a couple of hot spots on his rear end, tail, and leg. I had a monster hot spot of guilt on my own heart. Why had I been so self-consumed? Why hadn't I listened to that warning voice in my head? Why hadn't I at least called her doctor to express concern? Maybe Mom would have resisted a checkup and tests…but she might have agreed. And if she had, perhaps the heart attack could have been averted and she wouldn't be fighting for her life in the ER!

Amazingly, at the age of 90, Mom survived this near-death experience and a procedure to deal with some blocked arteries. And gradually, I let up on gnawing at my guilt hot spot. I understood that even though I blew it, God forgave me. I understood that Jesus died to cover my sins of selfishness and negligence (and all my others) with His blood. But the wound still burned with my own self-condemnation, and my impulse was to keep on licking. I had to fight this…and as Mom slowly seemed to improve, it got a bit easier to do.

I hoped the surgical procedure and Mom's follow-up medication and care would buy her an extra two or three years of life. It was not to be. Five months later she started going into repeated congestive heart failure. Her cardiologist told me her heart was tired and couldn't go on. With Mom's consent, she was put into hospice and died days later.

Needless to say, my guilt hot spot flared again. I was tempted to chew it into a red-hot boil. But I knew it wasn't what she would have wanted, or what God desired. I knew I needed to let God "cone" me anew with the pardon Jesus purchased, and gradually, I did. I have also tried to honor Mom's memory and use the resources she left me in ways that would please and honor her and my Lord.

Munchie the dog didn't realize gnawing at his hot spots would make them worse, not better. I did, but I still had to fight the impulse to do so. I have to think the apostle Paul might have faced the same struggle. His hot spot of guilt came from having persecuted the early church and having stood by while Stephen was martyred. But he also understood God's grace. That's why he wrote in 1 Timothy 1:13-14, "Even though I was once a blasphemer and a persecutor and a violent man, I was shown mercy because I acted in ignorance and unbelief. The grace of our Lord was poured out on me abundantly, along with the faith and love that are in Christ Jesus."

Munchie has been with me a year and a half now. He is owie-free. His shaved fur has grown back lush and plush. But he and my other four-foots still need their once-a-month flea treatment to keep the problem from recurring.

I also need ongoing "flea treatment" for the sins that try to jump on me and bite me and give me spiritual sores. I need to confess to God on an ongoing basis. And I need to receive the forgiveness He so freely gives—so I can be lush and plush in serving Him.

Let us draw near to God with a sincere heart and with the full assurance that faith brings, having our hearts sprinkled to cleanse us from a guilty conscience and having our bodies washed with pure water (Hebrews 10:22).

Consider This:

Have you ever kept picking at a wound of guilt? How did this impact your physical and emotional health? How did it affect you spiritually? Do you need to ask forgiveness of others and God, and let Him "cone" and heal you?

Gone with the Wyndy
Don't Be Deceived

Man's mind is so formed that it is far more
susceptible to falsehood than to truth.

Desiderius Erasmus

Geldenwynde Wilson was the registered name for Wyndy, a beautiful, well-trained four-year-old golden retriever. She belonged to Steven Wilson and his family. Wyndy loved her people and showed it in many wonderful canine ways. She slept when they slept. She always joined in when they sat together to watch TV. But her favorite thing was to play outside. She would fetch anything they threw for her, and return it with vigor. Of course, there were times when she would take the object to be fetched and run with it—as her people gave chase, yelling happily.

Quite often, Wyndy would also travel with the Wilsons. She seemed to enjoy it immensely. But on one particular occasion, the destination for their weekend trip was not suitable for dogs, so they left Wyndy home.

Wyndy's family put out a large bowl of food for her, because they knew she only ate when she was hungry. They filled a five-gallon bucket with water for her to drink. They left their old truck in the backyard so Wyndy knew they would not be gone permanently. That truck had been "hers" since puppyhood. Wyndy dug a hole beside the wheel to lie in and put a rag in it for a snuggle.

As they were leaving, the family hugged Wyndy and said goodbye. They thought they'd just be apart for a couple of days. But when they returned, Wyndy was nowhere to be seen.

The Wilsons checked the neighborhood. Wyndy was a friendly dog and everyone knew her. But their search came up empty. No one had seen her. They called the pound, but she was not there. Then they put up signs everywhere and waited anxiously for a response, praying their beloved Wyndy would be found.

A few days later, they got a phone call. A friendly female voice spoke to them. She said she thought she had the Wilsons' dog. Was it a beautiful golden retriever? Their answer was an eager, grateful *Yes*! The kind voice said the dog looked dirty, hungry, and tired— but well. Then the caller asked, "What is your dog's name?"

Steven was filled with excitement to think that Wyndy was finally found. He said the dog's name without thinking twice. He heard Wyndy's toenails clicking on the floor as he imagined her getting up to run to the phone in response to her master's voice.

The kind voice on the other end of the line called, "Here Wyndy, here girl!" Then the voice said, "Yep, this is her. Thanks!" The unknown person hung up and was never heard from again.

Wyndy's people were stunned. What they thought was a kind, friendly voice was really a deceiving, evil one. But, what could they do? They prayed again for Wyndy, but this time they prayed that her new family would love her and take good care of her.

Though the circumstances were different, my son, John, and some friends of his also wound up with someone who pretended to be other than he was. They were on a school band trip in Florida and had a free day to explore. A taxi-type car stopped in front of them and the driver told them to get into the car for a day of wonderful experiences. Although the man seemed safe enough, the boys declined and kept on walking. The man stuck with them and persisted in trying to change their minds. He said he could show them things they had never seen before. The boys continued to refuse. Finally the man said in a rather gruff voice, "Boys, get in the car." For whatever reason, they reluctantly gave in.

Their bogus "tour guide" showed them some sights, then took them to a bar where he told them they could drink without getting caught. The boys told him they weren't interested. They asked the man to take them back to the place where he'd picked them up. Instead, he took them to a tunnel and told them it was the end of the ride unless they gave him money. They refused. The man left them there—miles from where they needed to be. It took them most of the afternoon to get back. Fortunately, they made it—tired but safe—when so much harm could have come to them.

Like the person who took Wyndy, this man was a deceiver. At first, his offer sounded like it could be fun. But it didn't take long for John and his friends to realize that he was evil and they were in harm's way. I don't know if the boys prayed during the time they were in this man's clutches, but the whole trip was being constantly lifted up in prayer. Many parents, students, and friends were asking God to keep everyone safe, and I'm sure that's what kept them from a worse result.

Wyndy's family won't ever know the whole story of how she was taken. The woman caller said she'd found Wyndy out on the road. Maybe Wyndy was fooled by the woman's seemingly kind voice and went with her. She had never known anything but love and kindness. And perhaps the woman needed a dog so badly that she was willing to break the hearts of an entire family to fill her need. Nevertheless, it was wrong. And the man who lured the boys into his car may have been in it only for the money. But that was wrong too—and it was a terrifying experience for a few scared teenagers.

There is another way that we are all in danger of being deceived and lured by an imposter. Jesus spoke of it when He walked this earth. He promised He would come again, but first, false messiahs would try to get people to follow them instead. In Luke 21:8, He warned: "Watch out that you are not deceived. For many will come in my name, claiming, 'I am he,' and, 'The time is near.' Do not follow them."

Wyndy was taken many years ago, but the memory and hurt still linger, and she was gone forever. John and his friends escaped with just a scary afternoon. In the end, both Wyndy's family and the boys learned how easy it is to be deceived. But we don't need to get in the car with evil or be tricked into following false masters. If we stay alert to God's Word and ask Him for wisdom, He will guide us safely home to Him.

If any of you lacks wisdom, you should ask God, who gives generously to all without finding fault, and it will be given to you. But when you ask, you must believe and not doubt, because the one who doubts is like a wave of the sea, blown and tossed by the wind (James 1:5-6).

Consider This:

Have you ever been deceived by someone? What happened? What did you learn? What principles from God's Word might help protect you in the future?

The Dog Who Played with Fire
To Quench or Not to Quench?

Passion, though a bad regulator, is a powerful spring.
RALPH WALDO EMERSON

Lucy the border collie's favorite holiday was the Fourth of July. She wasn't particularly patriotic, but she was crazy about fire and fireworks. When a fuse was lit and her extended human family began the countdown, "Ten…nine…eight," Lucy's ears would perk up and she'd run in mad circles. "Three…two…one…BOOM!" Lucy's heart leaped in her chest as she witnessed the rockets' red glare and bombs bursting in air. But she wasn't content to be a passive observer like her people. Lucy would charge in and snap at the fireworks—and at times, the fireworks would snap back. These mini-burns never deterred Lucy. She'd shake her head, lick her chops, and go back to fire-snapping until all the sparkling flames were gone.

David can't remember a time when Lucy didn't have an affinity for fire. She was born with this hot-blooded trait. He thought it was either instinct—or foolishness. David's family owned two other dogs, a golden retriever and a chocolate Lab. Other than being annoyed by the noise, neither of them showed any interest in fireworks. The Fourth of July was just another day.

Lucy's other favorite celebrations were birthdays. David loved to watch Lucy's growing excitement when dinner ended and the cake was being prepared in the kitchen. As the candles were lit, the pyro-loving pup would crouch down and wait, occasionally running in circles, eagerly anticipating the explosion. Since David's family wasn't partial to trick candles, this moment never came. Still, Lucy never wavered from her passion. Even when she was lying in her whelping box surrounded by a litter of newborn puppies, if a flame was lit nearby she'd hop out and do her fire-snapping dance. Her maternal instinct was trumped by her desire for fire.

Lucy's interest in fire and fireworks wasn't something she picked up from the Dog Whisperer or in obedience school. No, her lifelong enchantment with fire was implanted by her Creator. The same God who knit you and me together in our mothers' wombs (Psalm 139:13) gave Lucy her unique fascination with flame.

Why?

It'd be nice if I could telepathically ask Lucy, "Why are you so passionate about fire?" Perhaps she'd given it some thought over the years and could articulate an insightful response—or maybe she'd simply shrug and telepathically answer, "I don't know. I just am."

Lucy and fire. God only knows. For us, there's no way to know why. It just is. Like the beautiful flowers that grow, bloom, and die on remote mountaintops or in virgin rainforests without ever once being seen by an appreciating human eye.

Why did God plant them there?

Of what purpose are these breathtaking flowers that never get seen or smelled? Of what purpose is a fire-snapping dog?

David and I discussed the matter. We couldn't come up with any explanations that held water. Lucy was no canine Smokey the Bear. She wasn't a descendent of any firehouse Dalmatians. So why did God make her that way?

While they didn't understand the why of it, Lucy's family still gave her every opportunity to exercise it. They didn't lock her up in the basement on the Fourth or exile her to the backyard during birthday parties. They weighed the pros and cons of her fire fascination and concluded that it brought joy to Lucy and wasn't harmful to her or others. David's family recognized Lucy's instinctive passion and rather than quench it, found safe outlets for her to enjoy what she loved. David said, "We always ensured Lucy was around whenever there was a fire to be had."

How many of us parents have watched a passion develop in our children in the same way? From early childhood, even in infancy, some kids are born with something they love more than anything else. Ever since my nine-year-old son discovered balls, he hasn't been able to get enough of kicking, throwing, bouncing, bowling, or spinning them. I'm not saying he's going to be a professional bowler or Ping-Pong player, but we try to give him ample opportunity to express his passion, whether it's in soccer, basketball, football, or baseball. I have another friend whose son was fascinated by classic monster movies ever since he was a tiny kid. He never lost that fascination and is now one of the youngest professionals in the field of monster movie make-up and masks. Albert Einstein recalled that when he was eight, he received a compass from his father. Albert was enchanted by the magnetic needle magically pointing north and something clicked in him. Unraveling the mystery behind the invisible force that made the needle move would become a lifelong obsession. (His study of electromagnetism figured into the theory of relativity—one of the greatest scientific breakthroughs of the twentieth century.)

Some people—and dogs—are born with specific passions. These weren't force-fed by parents or taught in school. Why did the Creator put them there? We'd have about the same luck telepathically asking God as we would that border collie—so thankfully God tells us why in the Bible.

First, we acknowledge that everyone is uniquely made by God.

Psalm 139:13: "For you created my inmost being; you knit me together in my mother's womb."

Second, just as David gave Lucy every opportunity to exercise her passion, so God wants the same for us. He designed us uniquely for a purpose. Read what Paul wrote in 1 Corinthians 12:17-18 (MSG): "If the body was all eye, how could it hear? If all ear, how could it smell? As it is, we see that God has carefully placed each part of the body right where he wanted it."

Feet, hands, ears, eyes. On their own, apart from the body, they have unclear or little purpose, but when placed by the Creator exactly where they're supposed to be and functioning in the way He designed, each part is indispensable.

Fire-snapping dogs, blooms that are never seen, little boys who love balls, movie monsters, and compasses. We mere dog owners and parents often don't see why we should encourage these passions. We don't understand why God made our dog or kids the way He did. It's not how we would design the perfect dog or child. But rather than quench what God in His wisdom has created, we can simply be good stewards of His creations and encourage healthy development of those passions, just as David and his family did with their pyro-fascinated pup.

Bottom line: the Creator knows why He gave certain people and pups the unique passions He gave them and sometimes He keeps the reasons to Himself. And after we tire of all the speculation and second-guessing of God, it simply comes down to Isaiah 45:15 (NLT), "Truly, O God of Israel, our Savior, you work in mysterious ways."

Oh, the depth of the riches of the wisdom and knowledge of God! How unsearchable his judgments, and his paths beyond tracing out! (Romans 11:33).

Consider This:

Do you have or know a child who has a strong passion for something? Has that passion been quenched or encouraged? How might you support its safe and wholesome expression? Did you yourself have an early passion? Was it supported? In what way is it still part of your life now?

Why Wally Bloomed
Talent Needs Nurture

*There are two lasting bequests we can give our
children: One is roots, the other is wings.*
HODDING CARTER

In Lili's family, dogs and kids went together like salt and pepper.
They were always spicing up each other's lives. But time was passing, and one by one Lili's children were heading off to college. Only
her youngest was left at home when their latest canine, an adorable but feisty border collie named Lizzie, ran out to the street and
was hit by a car.

Lili and her husband were devastated. All their children were
urging them to get another pooch, but Lili dragged her heels, not
quite sure God was leading this way. Finally she learned there were
puppies for sale at the end of her street. She decided to take a look.
There was just one left, a boy. Without giving it much thought, she
took the plunge. She named her new dog Wally.

Lili's little bundle of puppy love turned out to be spring-loaded
for bear. He was an Australian shepherd, a breed that ranks number eight in dominance on a scale of one to ten. These dogs are
herders. They crave activity. What Lili and her husband had was a
Lizzie personality in a male puppy's body. What they didn't have
was three active sons at home to run Wally's energy out of him.

They had one active daughter—but she would soon be following her brothers off to school.

Conscientious parents that they are, Lili and her hubby tried to do their best by Wally. They took him to puppy classes. When that wasn't enough, they got him private training. They invested more in Wally than they had in all their other dogs put together. And things still weren't quite working.

Christmas was coming. Right afterward, the family was flying to Australia for their eldest son's wedding. Lili worried about who could keep the puppy in their absence. She also realized that in just a few months, their daughter would graduate from high school and fly the coop. Their nest would be empty except for one less-than-controllable dog. Lili began to think about finding a different home for Wally. She chatted with a woman from a pet store. Next thing she knew, Wally popped up on a site for rescue dogs. They started getting calls about him from strangers. Finally, Lili told a family of four from San Diego that they could come and meet him.

The family drove for several hours to reach Lili's home. There were two children, a girl and a boy. The first thing Wally did was to knock the little girl over. He didn't mean any harm—it was just his rambunctious way. The ten-year-old wasn't hurt, but she started crying. Lili thought, "That's it! No way will they take this dog!"

They took him.

Wally drove off to his new life, which included a fenced yard and new doggie pals. One month later, his new family emailed Lili. They loved Wally! He was great! A few more weeks passed and the family touched base again. They said Wally was winning agility competitions. Next thing Lili knew, Wally was a champion. He even had his own website!

At this point, Lili's husband only half-jokingly barked, "You gave away a champion?" To which Lili woofed, "He would never have become a champion in this house!"

Years later, Lili explained to me that Wally taught her a vital lesson—one she'll never forget. Talent needs the right soil in which to bloom. It's crucial for the parents of dogs and children to provide that soil. Once Wally got the fertilizer he needed, he blossomed into a winner!

My friend Sheilah saw that same principle play out in her grandson's life. Raymond had real musical talent, but it hadn't been developed. The family didn't have the means to nurture Raymond's innate abilities.

In Los Angeles where they live, special magnet high schools are geared to specific areas of interest. When Raymond was completing eighth grade, Sheilah longed for him to get into a particular high school that focused on music education. But the time to apply had passed. Besides, the competition was stiff, and Raymond had no formal training. He couldn't even read music. He just had one small drum that he played on his own.

Sheilah loves Jesus. She knows He can do miracles if He chooses. She is also part of the leadership of my Bible study class. She shared her burden and we began to pray for a miracle for Raymond. Lo and behold, Raymond's dad decided to take off work one day and bring his son to the music magnet, even though the new school year was about to start.

Getting in at such a late date seemed impossible. But Raymond and his dad started talking to the school personnel. They were told to return the next day so Raymond could audition. Despite the lateness of the hour and Raymond's lack of formal training, he was accepted.

In this new, fertile musical soil, Raymond's talent exploded into bloom, just like Wally's had. Now he reads music. He plays in bands both in and out of school. For his last birthday he wanted a cymbal for his drum set, so Sheilah took her grandson to the music store. She found herself facing no less than a whole wall of cymbals.

She never dreamed there were so many different kinds. Raymond spent an hour testing them one at a time, then finally chose a cymbal he thought might give him just the sound he wanted. He took it home, tried it out, and pronounced it perfect.

The right nurture made all the difference to Wally's agility and Raymond's music. It's also crucial to help us bloom spiritually. Our perfect Heavenly Parent understands this and gave specific instructions to the Israelites about how to plant successive generations in this rich spiritual soil. In Deuteronomy 6:6-7 Moses says, "These commandments that I give you today are to be on your hearts. Impress them on your children. Talk about them when you sit at home and when you walk along the road, when you lie down and when you get up." God also gave the Israelites festivals to keep and pass on to their children to remind them of what He had done for them, and thereby grow their faith.

Dogs and children are a gift from God. When they blossom and grow, He is pleased. If you are a parent of either, in what soil will you plant the lives entrusted to you?

Do not exasperate your children; instead, bring them up in the training and instruction of the Lord (Ephesians 6:4).

Consider This:

Have you ever nurtured a pet's or child's talent? How did it help them blossom? What blessings did this bring? Who in your life might God be calling you to nurture spiritually?

Chasing Buggies
What Do You Pursue?

*Most people never run far enough on their
first wind to find out they've got a second.*

WILLIAM JAMES

There were certain things that riled up my dog Gracie. Things that either tempted her or bugged her so much that she'd jump up from whatever she was doing (usually napping) and bark her head off and give chase. Deer and UPS trucks topped her list. Every dog has its own particular triggers that set off such reactions.

With Pepper the Beagle from Pennsylvania it was…Amish buggies.

Alex and his dog Pepper grew up in Lancaster County, Pennsylvania, which has one of the largest concentrations of Amish in America. The farmhouse Alex lived in was like an island in an ocean of cornfields. The two-lane asphalt highway in front of the house was as neatly combed down the middle as if Moses had raised his staff and parted the corn himself.

Compared to LA freeways, this was a road much, *much* less traveled. On a good day nine or ten Amish buggies would pass by, and it seemed this is what Pepper lived for. The Beagle would go nuts, barking, chasing, and nipping after the horse-drawn vehicles.

Alex told me Pepper didn't bark at other cars or trucks. The Beagle wasn't particularly interested in horses or other farm animals. No, Pepper had a thing for Amish buggies. Whether they bugged her or turned her on, these buggies were Pepper's passion; perhaps stirred up by a repressed Beagle memory of a time when packs of prehistoric Beagles hunted down large, black, slow-moving dinosaurs. (Just a theory.)

To prevent Pepper from dragging home an Amish buggy and burying it on their property, Alex's parents began to tie up Pepper in the backyard whenever a buggy approached. Pepper could still see out onto the road and whenever the buggies passed by, she would bark her brains out—with the plastic leash in between her teeth. The more she barked, the more her sharp teeth would cut against the leash. This is proof that dogs know how to multitask. After a season of chewing and barking she'd break through the leash and take off after the buggy. Alex reported that Pepper probably went through one leash for each of her 14 years with their family. As to why they didn't buy a steel-chain leash, Alex shrugged, "The plastic ones were so much cheaper."

No doubt, Pepper had a lifelong obsession with Amish buggies. They riled her up from puppyhood through canine AARP. She always barked at them. Always chased them with all her heart. She patiently chewed, year after year, through leash after leash, to pursue her passion.

That's single-minded perseverance.

What are we willing to spend our whole life pursuing? And what goal ignites our passions such that we're willing to chew through countless entanglements of an insanely busy life to reach them?

I've spent a lot of my adult life writing screenplays that don't sell. I have chewed through years of disappointment and frustration in pursuit of my dream of having a major feature film produced—only to be stopped cold, dragged back into the yard, and leashed up again. And from my back-to-square-one position, I still have a painful view of all the Amish buggies passing me by, of missed opportunities and daily reports of others getting their films produced.

Yet year after year I persevere, I bark and chew and keep writing even when it hurts—because writing isn't something I do; it's who I am. It's my passion. Until God shows me otherwise, it's what I'll do until the day I die.

What is your God-given passion? That something that can't be superficially scraped off like frosting on a cake? What's your Amish buggy? What do you pursue that is powerfully instinctive and pri-mal; something you were born with; something God planted in the deepest part of you?

I believe we all have our Amish buggies.

Back in Old Testament times, Nehemiah had a passion to rebuild the wall of Jerusalem that had been destroyed by Nebu-chadnezzar and the Babylonians around 600 B.C. When Nehe-miah (cupbearer to the King of Persia) returned to his ancestors' homeland 150 years later to do what God put on his heart, he was met with opposition. He had finished most of the wall, but still had to hang the huge doors. His enemies conspired and sent him a message inviting him to a meeting. But Nehemiah didn't take their bait. He knew they meant him harm. They sent the same passive-aggressive message four times and each time Nehemiah sent mes-sengers with the same blunt response: "I am doing a great work and I cannot come down. Why should the work stop while I leave it and come down to you?" (Nehemiah 6:3 NASB).

Don't waste my time. Don't distract me from my heart's goal.

Don't get between me and my Amish buggy!

Nehemiah's enemies continued to put up more obstacles between him and the completion of the wall—but Nehemiah chewed right through them with Beagle-like persistence. The wall was completed in 52 days. It was an externalization of a passion, something quantifiable, like a chewed-up leash and a dog running after an Amish buggy.

But beneath the surface of external things, there is a deeper underlying internal passion that must be pursued no matter how busy we are, how tied down we are, whether young or old, sick or healthy, rich or poor. In 1 Timothy 6:11 we are told to "pursue righteousness, godliness, faith, love, endurance and gentleness."

Can you imagine what might happen if you pursued God and these God-given qualities with the same passion and perseverance that Pepper pursued her Amish buggies?

Nehemiah did.

Here's a little peek behind the scenes of the building project. It wasn't just a one-man job. Nehemiah also got a little help along the way! In Nehemiah 6:9 (NKJV) we hear him pray, "Now therefore, O God, strengthen my hands." And when the wall was completed in an impossibly short 52 days, Nehemiah lifted the curtain to reveal Who helped him achieve his heart's goal. (Hint: The same One who planted it there.) Nehemiah 6:16 (NASB) tells it like it is: "When all our enemies heard of [the completion of the wall], and all the nations surrounding us saw it, they lost their confidence; for they recognized that this work had been accomplished with the help of our God."

What if you took after Nehemiah and pursued your heart's passion and the God who planted it there—at the same time?

Whoever pursues righteousness and love finds life, prosperity and honor (Proverbs 21:21).

Consider This:

What do you pursue most passionately in life? What has been the result? Do you pursue God with the same passion? If not, what do you think might happen if you did?

Part IV

Tales to Lift Your Spirits

🐾 Katie 🐾

The Pup That Wouldn't Give Up
Persistence Pays

Fall seven times, stand up eight.
JAPANESE PROVERB

Katie is a beautiful little border collie that Duane and Cher Jost adopted from the pound. At first she was timid and cautious, but her family poured love on her and she opened up her heart to them. Katie is a very friendly dog and quickly became a favorite in their beautiful country neighborhood. She had an early morning routine of going across the street and greeting everyone as they went off to work or school. They all happily greeted her too and then lovingly shooed her back home.

One day a neighbor noticed Katie in her front yard, barking and jumping around as if she were on a mission. From her front door, the neighbor greeted Katie. Then she asked the dog to go home. Katie wouldn't budge. She kept persisting in whatever mission she was on. Finally the neighbor stepped outside to shoo Katie away. But the moment she turned back to the house, Katie started insisting again. This made the neighbor realize there might be something more to Katie's behavior. She started walking toward her barn. Katie ran circles around her and then darted toward the corral area. The neighbor suddenly noticed a newborn foal out by the road's edge. The foal had rolled under the fencing and was lying outside the corral area. Without help, the newborn could have died. But thanks to Katie's persistence, the neighbor found him and took care of him, and he was fine.

That day, Katie was hailed as the neighborhood hero. Even though she was already loved, she got even more genuine attention from the neighborhood folks from then on.

Katie's persistence saved the foal's life, but only because the neighbor responded. There was a choice involved. In my life, my doctor is persistent in giving me the right medications for my medical conditions. But if I chose not to take his advice, I could very possibly die. When I was having heart trouble my husband, Steve, was persistent in taking me to the doctor to be checked out. I told him I didn't have time to go to the doctor, but he insisted. The next day I had a quadruple heart bypass. Had Steve and my doctor not been persistent I would not be writing this story.

Back in the day when our children were young, during Vacation Bible School our home and car were always full of neighborhood kids. Some would stay for lunch and play. This gave them a chance to ask questions about the stories they had heard from the Bible, and it gave me a chance to talk to them more about Jesus. One particular young man would often stay in the kitchen with me after the others went out to play. We would talk about dogs or school or the swim team, but it would always end with him asking a question about the Bible. You could say I was persistent, but I would say that he was even more persistent in his questioning. Finally, one afternoon he decided to pray and ask Jesus to forgive his wrongdoings and to rule his life. He was probably in the fifth grade at this time. Now he is a grown man with a family of his own.

He loves the Lord and lives to please Him. His persistence paid off. He lives a full life here and will have eternal life in heaven.

Katie's persistence saved the foal's life. Steve's and my doctor's persistence saved mine. The young man's persistence in seeking God brought him life eternal. These are three proofs of Jesus's teaching and Paul's words in Galatians 6:9: "Let us not become weary in doing good, for at the proper time we will reap a harvest if we do not give up."

Forgetting what is behind and straining toward what is ahead, I press on toward the goal to win the prize for which God has called me heavenward in Christ Jesus (Philippians 3:13-14).

Consider This:

Have you ever struggled to persist in something and then seen your persistence pay off? What was hardest about keeping on? What was most rewarding about the end result? What did you learn that may help you persevere in the future?

The Facebook Bark
Communication Counts

The gospel is only good news if it gets there in time.
CARL F.H. HENRY

I love the classic Disney movie *One Hundred and One Dalmatians.* One of my favorite parts is the twilight bark. When the Dalmatian puppies go missing, their frantic doggie parents use a barking relay to search for them. News of their disappearance is woofed from one dog to another until finally, the puppies are found and eventually rescued from the villains who stole them.

Well, that particular brand of social networking was a figment of storytelling imagination. So when my dear friend Charlotte's toy Sheltie, Tess, went missing recently, she tried a Facebook bark instead.

Charlotte lives on a farm in South Carolina. She teaches horseback riding and raises toy Shelties. She adores every puppy born in her home and has a standing policy that any dog can be returned at any time for any reason if its family can no longer keep it.

Beautiful Tess was a dog that came back. Her family adored her, but factors came into play that made them conclude, after much agonizing, that it might be best to give her up. Charlotte was not only delighted to take her back, but decided to keep her permanently.

Charlotte welcomed Tess back on a Thursday. Two days later, she had a little horse show at her farm. Tess and the other dogs were let out to play in a fully fenced yard. At some point, Charlotte discovered to her horror that Tess was gone. A telltale hole suggested she'd dug her way under the fence and taken off.

No one knows for certain why Tess escaped. A likely guess is that she still wasn't quite sure where home was. It was a terrible time to be loose. A storm hit. Snow fell. It was freezing cold. To make matters worse, Tess had no collar or tags. Her return had been so recent that this little matter hadn't been attended to yet.

Charlotte networks on Facebook constantly and has hundreds of friends. Many live right in her area. Charlotte posted a plea for help. She got it! Tess's former family put up current photos of the dog. People cross-posted Tess's plight to spread the word. Countless Facebook pages trumpeted the missing dog alert. Posts also triggered massive prayers for Tess to be safe from the storm and be found. Charlotte and friends who lived nearby put up posters and launched a physical search—but the Facebook relay got the news out much more widely.

Across the country in California, I prayed too. Monday morning came. Still no Tess. Charlotte was hoping and praying she was somewhere safe and warm with humans who had taken her in with no way to know where she belonged. I prayed again and begged God she'd be located.

Then, I saw the post that made my day—someone thought they had her!

It was true! She'd been found and spent the weekend with a local family. They'd had no idea who her owners were. Monday they'd seen a Facebook alert about Tess and realized this was probably the dog they'd been falling in love with. A grateful Charlotte profusely thanked her new human friends and welcomed the little truant back into her embrace, praising God for answered prayer.

So, what's the moral of this story? Keep tags on your dog at all times? It's great to have friends? Prayer makes a difference? Those are valid lessons, yes. But this tale has deeper significance for me. It makes me think of my loving Lord who weeps over those who are spiritually lost. And it makes me realize the crucial importance of spreading the gospel's good news so they might hear and come home to Him.

In what's famously referred to as the Great Commission, Jesus said, "All authority in heaven and on earth has been given to me. Therefore go and make disciples of all nations, baptizing them in the name of the Father and of the Son and of the Holy Spirit, and teaching them to obey everything I have commanded you" (Matthew 28:18-20).

Long before Facebook and animated movies, Jesus was urging a communications relay to get out the word about Him. In the absence of modern media, God spread the gospel by spreading people. The early church in Jerusalem was scattered because of persecution, and the good news scattered right along with it. But each generation must get out the word anew.

Tess is home because people cared enough to spread the word about her plight. Are there people in your life who might come home to God if you helped to show them the way?

Consequently, faith comes from hearing the message, and the message is heard through the word about Christ (Romans 10:17).

Consider This:

Who in your life might need to find their way home to God? How might you relay the gospel to them? How could you participate in posting it more widely to other areas of the world?

Paper Dog Delight
Joy Is Contagious

Happiness held is the seed;
happiness shared is the flower.
ANONYMOUS

When he was a chubby, out-of-shape 14-year-old, Dean loathed being a paper boy. The last thing he wanted to do was go outside and exercise. Why ride a bike and fling papers day in and day out for slave wages when he could be sprawled on a couch watching TV or taking a nap?

Rags, Dean's Beagle/terrier mix, felt quite differently. His master's paper route was the highlight of this dog's existence. As Dean huffed and puffed along, laboriously tossing papers, Rags would romp joyfully alongside. Rags memorized the route and would dash ahead of Dean to identify the next house with all the exuberance of a bird dog pointing out the prey. For Rags, delivering papers wasn't an exhausting, low-paying job—it was fun! He delighted in it. What was drudgery for Dean was a blast for his dog. And now, many years later, when Dean recalls his paper route he no longer sees the experience through the eyes of his teenage self, but through his joyful memories of his beloved dog. Now a trim and fit adult, Dean admits that Rags and the paper route is probably the happiest memory of his fourteenth year. Such is the power of joy.

When you live in Southern California, one of the required rites of passage is introducing your child to Disneyland—"the Happiest Place on Earth." We first took our boy, Skye, when he was three. At his age and height—he was less than 36 inches tall—he wasn't allowed on the adult rides I considered more fun. So we stayed mostly in Fantasy Land, going on kiddie rides I faintly recalled experiencing with my parents when I'd been Skye's age. These were older, slower, gentler rides—less high-tech and with fewer thrills—rides I enjoyed for nostalgia's sake but not ones I'd have chosen if my wife, Celine, and I had been on our own. But it's not the attractions that make Disneyland so memorable—it's the joy on your toddler's face as he or she delights in flying over London with Peter Pan for the first time or holding on to a unicorn on a maiden spin around the merry-go-round.

When Skye was seven—old enough and tall enough to go on the adult rides—we took him to Disneyland again. While I still enjoyed riding the Matterhorn, my real kick was Skye asking if the Abominable Snowmen on the ride would be real—or the delight on his face when we got soaking wet on Splash Mountain and he wanted to go right back and do it all over again.

Rags and Skye both give examples of how the innocent joy of a dog or a child can transform the familiar, the mundane, even the dismal into a pleasant and positive memory. So, if a Beagle/terrier mix and a little boy have such power, how might we as children of God be able to transform the world around us?

Many people perceive the world they live in as familiar, mundane, and even dismal. If we who know the Lord were truly a delight and joy to be around, how might this affect their experience? If, in the face of negativity, we lived out the fruits of the Spirit, how might it turn their worldview upside down? If we delighted and rejoiced in the Lord, how might it transform their lives?

I once had a student tell me how much I'd impacted his life—based on a brief meeting we'd had on campus that I could barely remember. I was surprised when he said that. He saw our half hour together as a key moment, but I saw it as just hanging out with him. Perhaps I tossed out a nugget of wisdom or said an encouraging word or two. I can't recall. But like Rags and Skye weren't consciously trying to pump joy and positive vibes into their world, neither was I. Like Dean's dog and my son, I was just being.

It is the highest blessing in the universe to be children of God. As His children, we are urged in Psalm 37:4 to delight ourselves in Him. If we continually delight in the One who dwells in our innermost hearts, we cannot help but spread His joy and transform the world around us.

Shout for joy to the LORD, all the earth. Worship the LORD with gladness; come before him with joyful songs. Know that the LORD is God. It is he who made us, and we are his; we are his people, the sheep of his pasture (Psalm 100:1-3).

Consider This:

What are some of the most joyful moments of your life? What are some times you've delighted in the Lord? How did your joy affect those around you? How can you spread joy to those around you right now?

Marley and Goliath
The Small Can Be Mighty

It's not the size of the dog in the fight,
it's the size of the fight in the dog.

MARK TWAIN

Have you ever heard it said of people that they don't know their own strength? Well, my little puppy Marley doesn't know his own size. He was less than three pounds when he stood his ground with a full-grown pit bull and showed no signs of shrinking back.

Okay, so the pit bull was a pussycat…but how was Marley to know that? He had never met Sasha before. She was one of four dogs that belonged to his then-trainer, Sue. When Sue took Marley to her place for some extra homeschooling, she plopped him down with her brood and Marley never flinched.

Nor was Marley afraid to flex his pint-sized muscles with his new pit bull pal. When Sasha woke him up from a nap, he fussed at his oversized playmate. He started growling and biting at her mouth…and she took it!

That was all before Marley came to live with me. I don't have pit bulls—but I have a very large cat. Bo weighs three or four times what Marley did when he first arrived. Bo is also the bully of the household. If he wants me to himself, he'll whap any other four-foot aside to achieve his objective. Bo slapped Marley in this way. But tiny Marley also put the fear of dog into Bo. Not always, but sometimes, I would see my giant cat flee when Marley barked or ran at him. They like each other now, but I think my pint-sized puppy knocked Bo at least partway off his bully pulpit.

Marley is half papillon, a quarter toy Sheltie, and a quarter Pomeranian. Papillons have been dubbed big dogs in small dog bodies. Whatever the case, Marley's heart and courage are definitely huge for his size. I do believe he had some fear of my other four-foots, including Bo, when he first got here, but he didn't shrink back. He went full tilt to mark out his place in the family.

Marley's huge heart in a tiny body makes me think of a certain famous shepherd boy named David who faced off against a giant named Goliath. But there's a difference. David wasn't fighting to assert himself. He was fighting to uphold the name and honor of God. Even though humanly he was outmatched, he trusted God for the victory—and felled the giant with a slingshot and a stone.

Like so many Old Testament stories, David's battle with Goliath illustrates a deeper spiritual truth. God's children constantly battle spiritual Goliaths. They often pounce during tough times in life. And perhaps no life experience is more wrenching than the premature loss of a child—which is what my dear friend Lilly faced when her grandson was stricken with cancer.

Little Diego was only two when an extremely stubborn and aggressive form of cancer first reared its ugly head in his arm. His doctors tried chemo to save the limb. When that failed, they amputated his arm below the elbow to stop the cancer's spread. No go! The cancer attacked his brain and lungs. A huge community of believers fought for this child's life in prayer, and Diego valiantly soldiered on, playing pirate to symbolize his fight. But as his fifth birthday approached, things were looking grim. Grandma Lilly's heart was breaking.

A Goliath far worse than the ancient Philistine giant or even the cancer was stalking Lilly. This Goliath was the enemy of our souls. Satan wanted to use Diego's illness to attack Lilly's faith. But despite her agony, Lilly kept crying out to God—and He gave her the slingshot and stones she needed.

You might say that Lilly's slingshot was God's Spirit, God's Word, and the prayers of her friends. And yes, these were also stones to fling at Satan. But God chose some other special stones just for her. The first came in the form of a vision or dream. Lilly sensed God speaking to her and saying, "Give Me the child." She didn't want to. She struggled against it. But ultimately, she released her beloved Diego to the Lord. Then, in the vision, she saw her precious grandson running in a field. He had a full head of hair and both his arms—and he was laughing. Just weeks later, on Christmas Eve, five-year-old Diego went to be with Jesus.

The second special stone God gave Lilly to fight her Goliath didn't come till many months later. In the interim, Lilly battled depression. She struggled to believe God was good. Emotionally, she was riding a seemingly endless roller coaster of hurt and pain. But she refused to yield to Satan and jump off into unbelief. She clung to God instead.

Perhaps the toughest day of the year was Christmas Eve. Lilly wondered whether this treasured holiday would forever be darkened by the memory of Diego's death. Then, on the second anniversary of his passing, God gave Lilly a marvelous gift. Lilly's youngest daughter, Diego's aunt, phoned with the news that she was pregnant with her first child. She had purposely waited until Christmas Eve to share the news so her mom's painful memories would always be tempered by the joyous announcement of new life.

Marley has huge courage and spunk, and it serves him well on a doggie level. But some foes, like Lilly's, can't be defeated this way. Paul the apostle was thinking of just such Goliaths when he wrote, "Finally, be strong in the Lord and in his mighty power. Put on the full armor of God, so that you can take your stand against the devil's schemes. For our struggle is not against flesh and blood, but against the rulers, against the authorities, against the powers of this dark world and against the spiritual forces of evil in the heavenly realms" (Ephesians 6:10-12).

When David fought Goliath of old, he did it without physical armor. King Saul had offered his, but it didn't fit. God's spiritual armor, however, is one-size-fits-all. Lilly is wearing it and winning her battle. How about you?

Therefore put on the full armor of God, so that when the day of evil comes, you may be able to stand your ground, and after you have done everything, to stand (Ephesians 6:13).

Consider This:

Have you ever had to face a physical, emotional, or spiritual Goliath? How did you feel? What did you do? Who or what did you depend on? Do you put on God's armor on a daily basis? What difference has it made?

Short, But Not Shortchanged
God Sized Us for a Purpose

*Even the smallest person can change
the course of the future.*
J.R.R. TOLKIEN

Our dog Squitchey weighs just seven pounds. She looks like a Yorkie, but she acts like a Dalmatian. We found out she has both breeds in her lineage when my husband's sister had Squitchey's DNA analyzed as a birthday gift. She may be small, but she does her size proud. She holds her own with our Welsh corgi, Stuart, who is four times her weight. He is the alpha dog between them, but if he doesn't share quickly enough, she fights for her rights in playful, vigorous ways.

Thanks to her compact size, Squitchey can easily dig her way out from under the fence in our backyard. She doesn't go far; she seems to want to guard our home. She tries to walk quickly around it and then crawl back under the fence before we see her. When we do catch her, my husband, Steve, immediately fills up her latest hole with rocks and dirt. It doesn't seem to bother her. She just waits for the next opportunity and digs her way out at another place.

Squitchey's favorite thing to do after a long day of protecting is to jump up on Steve's lap as he sprawls in his easy chair. Much as she loves acting like a big dog, she seems to enjoy and appreciate the comfort of being small. Stuart tries to jump on laps too, but when he lands, he feels more like a bulldozer than a dog.

As canines go, Squitchey is short stuff. As humans go, so am I. Two of my very special friends are much taller than I am. That's not saying a lot considering I am only five feet, four inches—but Cory and Susie are both several inches taller. When we go places together, I often wish I were as tall as they are so I could get into tall vehicles without help. As it is, they hop into Susie's pickup and then drive to the curb where I am standing so I can climb in.

I've also wished I were tall enough to reach items on a high shelf by myself. I've had to ask for help to get a glass out of Susie's cupboard. Since I'm also arthritic, moving is even a challenge for me. Squitchey can jump four times her height and run in circles forever, but if I turned around too fast, I'd fall down.

But even though I'm vertically challenged and can't move as fast as Squitchey does, I can still get quite a bit done in a day. Then, at night, my favorite place to be is snuggled next to Steve for a peaceful sleep.

Being short and loving Steve's company is pretty much the extent of the likeness between Squitchey and me. But God made each of us the way we are for His purposes. Squitchey will remain close to seven pounds for the rest of her life. If she were a Dalmatian, she might not be the sweet little lap dog that she is. I could complain about my height, but doing so wouldn't change a thing. And who knows? God might have something special for me to do that I couldn't if I were tall.

That was certainly the case for a man named Zacchaeus. What he's best known for is being a "wee little man." He was also rich and an unscrupulous tax collector. God made him a little guy so He could emphasize this man's huge desire to see Jesus. In Luke

19, we read that Zacchaeus was so anxious to see the Lord that he climbed up into a sycamore tree so he could look over the crowd's heads. Jesus saw Zacchaeus's great longing and told him, "Zacchaeus, come down immediately. I must stay at your house today" (Luke 19:5). Zacchaeus repented of his cheating ways and followed Jesus. This short man's story has a big place in the Bible to this day.

Squitchey acts like a big dog at times, but she also enjoys her diminutive size, and it makes her a perfect lap dog. Being short doesn't mean God shortchanged me or Squitchey, or Zacchaeus, either. He made each of us unique and for a unique purpose—and no matter what our size, we can stand tall in our hearts knowing we are His creation.

I praise you because I am fearfully and wonderfully made; your works are wonderful, I know that full well (Psalm 139:14).

Consider This:

In what ways—height or others—do you feel shortchanged? How have you seen God use who you are for His unique purposes? Are you standing tall in your heart as His unique creation? If not, will you ask Him to help you do so?

The Gospel According to Munchie

The Price Must Be Right

It is true, Christian, the debt you owe to God must be paid in good and lawful money, but, take comfort. Here Christ is the paymaster.

WILLIAM GURNALL

My adorable nine-year-old papillon mix, Munchie, came to me from a rescue group. He was a pet whose person could no longer care for him. He wound up in an animal shelter where he was spotted by the head of this rescue group, Angie.

Angie realized this sweet little guy was a perfect candidate to be re-homed. He didn't even seem to realize he was in a shelter. She was determined to find him a new family. After a standard waiting period, she could pay a fee to get him out. The cost of Munchie's redemption was one hundred dollars. If it wasn't paid, he'd eventually be euthanized.

There was no way a dog could come up with one dollar, let alone one hundred. Munchie could not possibly have freed himself. He wouldn't even have understood that this was necessary. Fortunately, Angie had a heart to help him and was willing to do for him what he couldn't do for himself. The moment he became available she paid the price, took him from the shelter, and placed him in foster care. Some weeks later I took over his foster mom duties and ultimately adopted Munchie into my four-footed family.

Not long after Munchie's adoption, I had another, very different experience that underlined the importance of redemption. I was driving to meet some friends connected with a ministry about an hour from my home. The final portion of the trip involved taking a toll road. I was told the fee would be one dollar, and I made certain I had dollar bills available to pay.

I am not used to taking toll roads and I wasn't quite sure what to expect. But I assumed I'd drive up to a booth and give my money to a person. That's what I'd seen on toll roads in other parts of the country. This was not the case here, however. The booth was at the end of the road and there was no human in sight. A machine took the payment, and it only took coins. There was no barrier to keep a car from driving through without paying. But there was a prominent warning sign. It explained that there was a camera recording the cars that passed through, and the fine for failing to pay was 55 dollars.

I was stunned. I scrounged in my purse and didn't come up with anything close to a dollar in coins. I put my car in park and ran back to a vehicle that had pulled up behind me. I asked the driver if he had a dollar in change to trade for my bill. But he'd been caught by surprise as well, and was scrounging for coins himself.

I rushed back to my car and dug deeper. Somehow I found 60 cents. One dime fell from my hands to the driver's side floor mat. Just then the other driver appeared at my window saying he could give me 35 cents. But that was all he had to spare. I retrieved the fallen dime…but was still a nickel short. I'm sure I was praying as I dug some more. Miraculously, I found the last nickel.

I can't describe the relief that washed over me as I threw all my coins in the slot, watched the light turn green, and sped off down the ramp to my friends. Just like my dog, I couldn't have redeemed myself. Thankfully, God brought another driver who could supply exactly what I lacked to save me from the hefty fine I would have been assessed.

As I reflected on these two incidents, I realized they had some significant things in common. In both instances, there was a set price for redemption. In both instances, outside help was needed to pay. And for this reason, both situations offer an earthly window into a far greater heavenly truth—that we need a Savior to pay the price for our sin.

According to Hebrews 9:22, "The law requires that nearly everything be cleansed with blood, and without the shedding of blood there is no forgiveness." In Old Testament times, God's people observed a complicated system of animal sacrifice. But this payment only served as temporary redemption. New sins required new sacrifices.

Not so the sacrifice of God's Son. When Jesus, our Messiah, the Lamb of God, gave His sinless life for our sins, it redeemed us once and for all time—if we put our faith in Him. Hebrews 9:11-12 explains, "When Christ came as high priest of the good things that are now already here, he went through the greater and more perfect tabernacle that is not made with human hands, that is to say, is not a part of this creation. He did not enter by means of the blood of goats and calves; but he entered the Most Holy Place once for all by his own blood, thus obtaining eternal redemption."

When Munchie was redeemed from that shelter, he still couldn't care for himself. He needed a loving master to nurture him. Angie made certain this need was met and I am privileged to be Munchie's new human mommy and adoring caregiver. When I was redeemed from sin by faith in my loving Messiah, He led me to believers who could nurture me and grow me in my faith. He is still providing for my spiritual nurture—and using me to provide it for others.

Angie delights in saving dogs from death and placing them in loving families. God delights in saving us and adopting us into His. Have you let Him redeem you so you can spend eternity in His care?

> *For the wages of sin is death, but the gift of God is eternal life in Christ Jesus our Lord (Romans 6:23).*

Consider This:

When was the last time someone did something for you that you couldn't do for yourself? How did it help you? How did it affect your relationship with that person? How does that help you understand what Jesus did for you?

The Best Gift Ever
Receive and Rejoice

Giving is true having.
CHARLES HADDON SPURGEON

Christa's father had endured an emotionally difficult year. He'd lost a best friend to cancer. A friend's marriage had imploded. And when his beloved five-year-old Jack Russell terrier was stricken with a degenerative neck injury, he was the one who took Sammy to the vet to be put down. It was especially painful because Sammy was a lap dog and Dad's lap was Sammy's lap of choice to curl up on.

Christa and her family knew Dad was in a season of loss and grieving, so when Father's Day loomed on the horizon, it was imperative to find an uplifting present. They wanted something that would lift his burdens and bring a long-term smile to his face. Up until now, tools had always been the gift category that never failed to please Dad. Screwdriver sets, drills, and saws had been greatly appreciated over the years. But now Dad had every tool he needed. And the hardware store had yet to carry a reliable tool to chase away the blues.

On the day Sammy was put down, Christa's mom was at the drug store buying Dad a pet sympathy card when the check-out clerk asked about her loss and mentioned that her dog had recently given birth to a beautiful litter of shih tzu/Maltese-mix puppies— perhaps just the solution for Dad's empty lap syndrome. Intrigued, Mom viewed photos of the puppies on the clerk's cell phone right there at the register. They were adorable! Available for Father's Day delivery too. A few hours later, while Dad took a nap, Christa, her younger brother, and mom snuck out of the house to visit the puppies in person. It was love at first sight. Even the younger brother who'd been opting for a Rottweiler was won over. They all agreed: the lone little boy in the litter could be the perfect Father's Day gift for Dad.

Could be, not would be. It wasn't a sure thing. Christa and her family had a few details to mull over. They wanted to surprise Dad, but what if he didn't like this puppy? What if the puppy didn't like him? They hadn't discussed getting a new dog as a family. What if, after losing Sammy, Dad wasn't ready for a replacement?

Christa considered showing her dad the pictures. She thought about having him accompany them to look at the puppies and make his own choice. But finally, they decided that surprise was to be a crucial element of this Father's Day gift.

Christa's mom emailed the three other siblings who were no longer living at home. Everyone agreed the boy was the one. They all pitched in money to share the cost of the new puppy and hoped and prayed he would be right for Dad.

On Father's Day, while Dad was still asleep, his family woke up at 6:00 a.m. and tiptoed out to gather the dog, bed, and food. With the puppy safely concealed in a picnic basket under a mound of fabric, they snuck everything under the kitchen table before Dad awoke. The tension was as thick as a special ops military maneuver, especially with worrying whether or not this puppy would bark and ruin the surprise. Mom made Dad a cup of coffee as the kids led him into the kitchen. As he sat down, he quizzically looked under the table at the picnic basket. That's when it jumped, and Dad made eye contact with his Father's Day gift peeking out from under the red and white gingham. All he could say was, "How amazing!" He picked up the furry little guy and put him on his lap. Perfect fit. As the out-of-town kids phoned home, Dad said the same thing he said to those at the house, "It was the best gift ever!"

The newest member of this coffee-loving family was soon christened Maxwell Starbucks Evans III (Max for short).

The best gift ever!

Christa's family was amazed at how a tiny little guy like Max could lift a weight not even a forklift could budge—Dad's downcast spirit and heavy heart. The family thanked God for the miracle of a puppy.

Likewise, God sent another "tiny" miracle to lift off the immeasurable burden of sin from the human race. In His wisdom, God didn't materialize His only Son, Jesus, into the world as a sandal-wearing, bearded adult, but as an innocent little baby in a manger.

Like a puppy in a picnic basket.

Like the reason we celebrate Christmas.

The best gift ever!

Then the angel said to them, "Do not be afraid, for behold, I bring you good tidings of great joy which will be to all people. For there is born to you this day in the city of David a Savior, who is Christ the Lord. And this will be the sign to you: You will find a Babe wrapped in swaddling cloths, lying in a manger" (Luke 2:10-12 NKJV).

Consider This:

What is the best gift you've ever received from another human being? Who gave it to you? What made it so special? How did it affect your life? Have you ever received the best gift ever from God?

God's Plum Jam
Mix Some Sweet with the Bitter

Kind words can be short and easy to speak,
but their echoes are truly endless.

Mother Teresa

I shed actual tears of laughter over a humorous tidbit of writing that made the rounds on the Internet years ago. It was about how to give a cat a pill. In the course of multiple tries, the house and the human were wrecked, and the pill never did go down. This delightful essay ended with how to give a dog a pill—just wrap it in something tasty and it's gobbled right up.

Alas, when my little Pomeranian, Becca, got a tooth root abscess, my vet prescribed a liquid medication.

My initial, clumsy efforts to administer this liquid with a dropper threatened to give me a cat-type experience with my dog. I tried to force the dropper into her mouth and she freaked out. I may have gotten a little bit of liquid into her, but clearly this was not going to work. I called the vet's office and begged for a pill substitute. They said they'd arrange it.

Then, I had a sudden revelation. Maybe something sweet would help the liquid medication go down. I had a little plum jam in the fridge. I knew grapes and raisins were toxic to dogs, but plums weren't on the poison list. And the jam was sweetened with sugar rather than something like xylitol, which can be fatal to dogs in even tiny amounts. Maybe I could mix Becca's medicine with a dab of this jam and get her to lick it off the bottom of her dish. I administered the next dose this way…and Becca slurped it right up.

This experience taught me a lot about myself. I had gone into authoritarian mode, focusing only on the task of getting the needed medicine down Becca's throat. I hadn't stopped to think how rough and scary this must feel to her—and my own fears about her fighting the dropper made my efforts needlessly clunky. Once I took a step back, I realized there was a kinder, gentler way to get the task accomplished. That little bit of sweet changed the taste of her medicine just enough that my dog licked it up happily and without the stress.

I have experienced this plum jam principle in my own life too. In my case the medicine was career-related. Years ago I wrote for animated television shows. At one point, I was on staff with a major studio. I was blessed to have a story editor supervising me who had not only won numerous awards, but was a marvelous mentor. I was struggling, though. I felt frustrated and inadequate. I was terrified of failure. Not just my job, but my self-esteem, hung in the balance. This was not an optimal emotional place from which to learn.

My mentor was an encourager. One day, he said something to me that was balm to my battered self-image. He had been pleased by the emotional thrust of one of my stories. He told me I had the heart to do this kind of writing—and the rest could be learned. Those words of kindness and encouragement were like plum jam. They cut the bitter taste of how much I still had left to work on—and gave hope and the will to go on.

Becca needed physical medicine. I needed my writing skills to be doctored. We all need spiritual dosing from our Great Physician on a daily basis. Though Jesus paid for our sins on the cross and we are forgiven through faith in Him, life on earth is an ongoing process of having our spiritual warts removed by a loving and caring God. At times, that process can be much more bitter and painful than we'd like. But in His marvelous grace, God has given us plum jam to help us through. He has given us His Word and His Spirit, not only to guide and refine us, but to comfort us. But that's not all! Check out the plum jam in Hebrews 4:14-16: "Therefore, since we have a great high priest who has ascended into heaven, Jesus the Son of God, let us hold firmly to the faith we profess. For we do not have a high priest who is unable to empathize with our weaknesses, but we have one who has been tempted in every way, just as we are—yet he did not sin. Let us then approach God's throne of grace with confidence, so that we may receive mercy and find grace to help us in our time of need."

Becca didn't get any less medicine because it was mixed with plum jam. If anything she got more—because she didn't fight it. For her, this made the dosage easier to swallow. It was easier for me to swallow tough critique when it was sweetened by the plum jam of heartfelt encouragement. We all need the plum jam of God's grace and mercy when we hit a spiritual wall, and in Jesus we have a High Priest who can give each of us just the individual touch we need to keep walking with Him.

God wants us to be His instruments to soothe and encourage others too. He wants us to be spreaders of His plum jam. Is there someone you can encourage and uplift today?

*For everything that was written in the past was written
to teach us, so that through the endurance taught in*

the Scriptures and the encouragement they provide we might have hope (Romans 15:4).

Consider This:

Has anyone ever added plum jam to a bitter pill you had to swallow? Did it make things better? How? Have you ever done this for someone else? What happened?

Dog of Good Cheer
God Comforts Us

Your sorrow itself shall be turned into joy. Not
the sorrow to be taken away, and joy to be put in
its place, but the very sorrow which now grieves
you shall be turned into joy. God not only takes
away the bitterness and gives sweetness in its place,
but turns the bitterness into sweetness itself.

CHARLES HADDON SPURGEON

Nadja and her younger brother and sister were adopted from Russia when she was five years old. Her adoptive parents brought them from a sad, lonely existence to a warm, loving, Christ-centered home. Adopting all three of them allowed the children to comfort each other as they learned the ways of this new world. And their new parents gave them unconditional love.

But about one year after they were adopted, they had to deal with a new loss. Their adoptive daddy died of cancer. Everyone was stricken with grief.

One day Nadja's mom and uncle took the kids to see some golden retriever puppies. They ran all over the yard playing with their new four-footed friends, everyone smiling once again. They were told this was just a visit, but they could come back someday soon. Then they went back to their uncle's home for dinner.

Nadja's mom and uncle said they had to go to the store for something and would be right back. They left the children with other family members. When they returned, something was wriggling under Uncle's shirt. Out came a happy, squirming golden retriever puppy—just for them. Now it was their turn to adopt. Rosie became a beloved member of the family.

Their new dog proved a great addition. They were joyful once more as they played with Rosie, hugged her, and cuddled with her while they read or watched TV. Rosie was a great comfort to Nadja. When sadness or loneliness swept her soul, she invited Rosie up on her lap. They would sit together as Nadja held her close. Rosie's canine love was not a replacement for Nadja's father, but it helped tremendously to fill the huge hole that had been left first by the loss of her birth parents, and then by the death of her American dad who loved her so very much.

Nadja had some tough times growing up. But her American mom was there for her and her brother and sister. Mom loved them dearly and also taught them about Jesus's love, which is infinitely greater even than her own.

Part of that love involved discipline. Nadja learned about obedience from both her mom and her dog. Rosie wasn't too good at minding the children, but when Mom came into the room Rosie ran to her, sat down, and waited for instruction. She knew Mom was boss. She also learned that if she was obedient, doggie biscuits were in her near future.

Nadja's mom enrolled the children in a private Christian school where I was teaching at the time. She hoped it would help them adjust to their new culture more easily and also learn more about the love of Jesus. I had Nadja in my class. At one of the chapel services, the school presented all three kids with an American flag that had been flown over the White House. Their mom was so pleased. She hugged us with tears in her eyes.

That was about twelve years ago. Lately I've been going to a special pool to swim for therapeutic exercise. The other day I was introduced to a new swim coach. She was tall, slender, and beautiful and her name was Nadja. I looked at her and had to ask, "Are you from Russia?" She said yes. Then I asked if she had gone to Heritage Christian School. She had. I told her I was Mrs. Fleishauer, her third grade teacher. She gasped, "Oh my gosh! Yes you are!"

You just don't expect to see your third grade teacher in a swimsuit. We had switched roles. Now she was my instructor. It was obvious to me as we talked that Nadja had grown up not just physically, but spiritually as well. She shared with me that she had a personal relationship with the Lord and would soon be attending a Christian college.

I know Rosie was a great instrument of comfort for Nadja's family. Nadja was really little then, but she remembers how much she loved Rosie and that Rosie loved her. She recalls how comforting it was to have Rosie close to her when she was frightened or lonely. But, like her birth parents and her American dad, Rosie wouldn't be around to do that for her forever.

Jesus will! Nadja's relationship with Rosie was like a prelude in a very small way to how she felt when she accepted Jesus as her personal Savior. She accepted God's invitation to sit in His lap of comfort and strength, and she can go there always.

Many centuries ago, the apostle Paul also had some tough times. He suffered horrible persecution and severe physical hardships for his faith. But he also found great comfort in God's lap. That's why he could write, "Praise be to the God and Father of our Lord Jesus Christ, the Father of compassion and the God of all comfort, who comforts us in all our troubles, so that we can comfort those

in any trouble with the comfort we ourselves receive from God"
(2 Corinthians 1:3-4).

God invites all who will come to climb on His lap and receive
His comfort and goodness. Paul and Nadja said yes. Have you?

*My comfort in my suffering is this: Your promise preserves
my life (Psalm 119:50).*

Consider This:

*What persons or pets have been most comforting to you in
tough times? How did they make you feel better? How has
God been a source of comfort and strength?*

Munchie Gets a Leg Up
Answer God's Help Wanted Ad

God has not called us to see through each
other, but to see each other through.

Munchie, my little papillon mix, is the stockiest dog I've ever had. He's also the least athletic. In their prime, all the others could easily leap up onto my king-sized bed. They adored snuggling and cuddling there, and I adored their soft warmth and affection. When Munchie joined my four-footed family, his fondest wish was to enter into the lovefest. But he didn't quite trust that his little legs could jump that high. And whether what he lacked was faith or spring, he usually couldn't make it.

I didn't want to overly baby the new dog in the pack. I felt that with encouragement, he could take this leap. Munchie loved food and I used treats to try to coax him to jump higher. He did manage to make it onto the bed now and then, but usually he came up short. Frantic to join us, he'd paw furiously at the bed's edge while loudly proclaiming his doggie frustration and begging for help. At this juncture, I sometimes just gave in and lifted him up. But I wasn't completely happy with this solution, and some furniture in my bedroom suggested another approach.

I have an easy chair in the room with a separate ottoman. I decided to scoot it next to the bed. With this assist and some coaxing from me, Munchie managed to get up on the bed on his own.

Okay, true confession time. I didn't persist in my ottoman solution. It's a bit heavy, and pushing it over grew tiresome. I got lazy, abandoned the practice, and went back to lifting Munchie onto my bed at night.

No matter. I think that ottoman exercise was more for me than my dog. God has shown me that at times, I expect too much of people. He has turned my experience with Munchie into a metaphor for that. On at least one occasion, He has literally whispered to my heart, "They can't jump from the floor to the bed. They need an ottoman." And I knew He wanted me to provide it.

I believe this metaphor has wider applications too. I've recently had the joy of becoming acquainted with a marvelous organization called Free Wheelchair Mission. They design simple, durable wheelchairs that cost roughly $50 to $60 each. Over the past ten years, they have given away half a million of these chairs to the poorest of the poor in countries all over the globe. These chairs have lifted crawlers off the ground, freed shut-ins to venture outside their homes, and in some cases made it possible for people to go to school or hold a job who couldn't have otherwise.

In April of 2010, I was privileged to travel with this organization to Chile. Seven of us flew from the U.S. and teamed with their distribution partners in Chile, FEDES Foundation, to give out a number of wheelchairs personally to prescreened recipients. They all had touching stories, but one young man in particular grabbed my heart.

This young man, roughly 30 years old, could not speak—he could only make sounds. A childhood illness had left him unable to walk. He had had a very rough life. But despite it, he had an indomitable spirit. He was clearly beyond grateful for the wheelchair and embraced it, eagerly soaking up our team's tips on how to drive it. We had the sense that he was eager for any small chance to be more independent…and would seize any opportunity he was offered.. As we pulled away in our car, he was wheeling his brand new chair up the street.

One of the Americans could not get this fellow out of her mind. Could more be done for this young man? Through a series of events, and with help from the wonderfully caring Chilean distribution partners, a special school was found for this worthy fellow. It is especially for young adults with disabilities. With financial help from his American sponsor, this young man is now being helped there.

But that's not the most amazing part of the story. His school evaluation revealed that this man's physical condition was deteriorating. Without therapy, he would soon have been unable to sit in his new wheelchair. The interested American had no clue about this, but God knew! God knew this young man needed a second "ottoman." Because a stranger answered the help wanted ad God placed on her heart, this fellow is now receiving much-needed therapy at the school, and both he and the "ottoman-giver" feel blessed.

Free Wheelchair Mission doesn't just distribute wheelchairs. They do it in God's name. They tell recipients their chair is from God, because He loves them. Their prayer is that the chairs not only open doors to greater physical mobility, but to a relationship with the Lord as well.

I am reminded of a certain cripple in Jesus's day whose physical infirmity also brought him to the Lord. He, too, got an "ottoman" from his friends. Mark 2:3-5 tells us, "Some men came, bringing to [Jesus] a paralyzed man, carried by four of them. Since they could not get him to Jesus because of the crowd, they made an opening in the roof above Jesus by digging through it and then lowered the mat the man was lying on. When Jesus saw their faith, he said to the paralyzed man, 'Son, your sins are forgiven.'"

I doubt forgiveness of sins was the goal this man and his friends were consciously seeking. Nor did it sit well with the watching religious elite. It sounded like blasphemy to them. So Jesus threw in the physical healing to prove His spiritual authority, and told the man to get up and walk—which he did.

As Munchie's loving master, I need to help him grow and learn and offer him an ottoman when he needs a leg up. God does the same for us, but not always directly. He often chooses to work at least partially through His children, like He did with the paralytic and the young man from Chile. God gives us the incomparable privilege of providing ottomans in His name. Will you listen for His help wanted ad and answer His call on your heart?

Then the righteous will answer him, "Lord, when did we see you hungry and feed you, or thirsty and give you something to drink? When did we see you a stranger and invite you in, or needing clothes and clothe you? When did we see you sick or in prison and go to visit you?" The King will reply, "Truly I tell you, whatever you did for one of the least of these brothers and sisters of mine, you did for me" (Matthew 25:37-40).

Consider This:

Has someone ever given you an "ottoman"? What was it? How did it help you? How did it affect your faith in God? Has God ever posted a help wanted ad in your heart? Did you answer it? If so, how was that a blessing?

Tag, You're It

How Does God Speak to You?

Every happening, great and small, is a parable whereby God speaks to us, and the art of life is to get the message.
MALCOLM MUGGERIDGE

Peter took his golden retriever, Bob, on regular hikes in the local mountains. Bob was fitted with a canine backpack to carry his water bottles, water dish, and dog snacks. If there was any room left over, Peter managed to sneak in a few of his own items.

Bob's backpack had pouches on the sides with two-way zippers that opened or closed in both directions. Peter made sure the zippers were pulled shut to the rear, not the front. Bob liked to go off-leash and explore on his own. If the zippers were closed to the front, they could snag on the brush and be pulled open and spill their contents.

Of course, one day Peter unintentionally shut the zippers in forward position. During the hike, Bob took off into the hills. When his dog returned, Peter noticed all the zippers pulled open. The water bottles were gone...as well as his car keys.

But it wasn't the missing keys that had Peter so upset. It was what was attached to his keys. It was the loss of a memento he had carried with him ever since he signed up for the military in 1959: his U.S. Army dog tag.

This little rectangular piece of stainless steel stamped with his name and number had been a part of him for over 50 years. He always carried it with him. And now that it was gone, he was furious. If Peter were a crusty curmudgeon cartoon character he'd have gone beet red with steam hissing out of his ears. He took a quick mental inventory of his worldly possessions and that dog tag topped the list of things he'd be devastated to lose.

After the initial shock wore off, Peter had only one mission: find that dog tag! He scoped out the area that Bob would've covered in his wanderings and systematically scoured every inch of dirt, brush, and rock. Peter emotionally flogged himself for zipping the pouches the wrong way. He checked, double-checked, and triple-checked the area, looking for any clue that could help, like a telltale water bottle or dog dish.

Hours later, hands and arms scratched by thistles and thorns, covered with dust and sweating like he'd been in a sauna, Peter was ready to give up. He was disgusted, frustrated, and broken. He was 99 percent sure he'd never find that very special part of himself that he had lost.

While Peter was experiencing a form of hell on earth, Bob seemed totally unaware. He was still in dog heaven, enjoying the outdoors, sniffing and rooting around for endless canine pleasures and treasures.

Then, at the precise moment when the proverbial last straw landed on Peter's back, when he conceded the dark forces of the universe had won, when he was 100 percent sure he'd never see his dog tag again—

Bob sat down.

Bob hadn't sat down once during the whole search. He'd been

a perpetual motion machine. Now at rest, Bob looked up, smiling at his exasperated and broken master.

Peter took a step toward Bob, then glanced down at the space between him and his golden retriever. There, at his feet, completely exposed and glistening in the sun lay—

The dog tag and keys!

It was utterly baffling how he could've missed them. He had searched this exact area multiple times. He bent down and picked up his keys and dog tag to make sure it was solid, his name stamped in metal, not some devilish illusion.

Then there was Bob. Peter looked at him, as if waiting for Bob to explain what had just happened. But Bob continued to gaze at Peter with that goofball grin dogs wear to cover up the possibility they're a lot smarter and wiser than we give them credit for.

The thought crossed and re-crossed Peter's mind. Did this dog know all along?

Peter vaguely remembers throwing a "what the heck" glance heavenward—not because he believed in God, but perhaps from years of cultural conditioning. People in the movies always glance upward after witnessing a miracle, right?

Peter has never been a religious man. He avoids church like soldiers avoid minefields. He doesn't pray to God, read the Bible, or sing worship songs in the car. Peter has never had a supernatural or spiritual moment in his life. That is, not until this incident with his dog tag and a golden retriever named Bob. Peter felt incredible relief being reunited with his precious dog tag. At the same time, it was spooky; downright "Twilight Zoney." And he'll be the first to admit that it made him acknowledge the possibility of God.

Could it be that ol' Bob knew something Peter didn't know? Could it be that dogs see things we don't see and hear things we don't hear? Could it be that the realm God resides in is outside the reality of man's five senses—but it's there?

The spiritual dimension is not the natural world we see, hear, feel, touch, and taste. It is a supernatural world we can only catch fleeting glimpses of, like a shadow seen out of the corner of your eye that vanishes when you turn to face it. For some, that glimpse of eternity may come through a great sermon, or meditation on a Scripture, or by being swept up in a divinely inspired song. But God doesn't always speak to people through pastors, TV evangelists, or the Bible on CD. God speaks to some of us in creative, nontraditional ways. He'll do whatever it takes to get our attention.

The apostle Peter was afraid to be associated with Jesus after He was arrested. Peter denied even knowing his Lord. God spoke to Peter through a bird. "And immediately the rooster crowed the second time. Suddenly, Jesus' words flashed through Peter's mind: 'Before the rooster crows twice, you will deny three times that you even know me.' And he broke down and wept" (Mark 14:72 NLT).

The Old Testament prophet Balaam was trying to force his donkey to carry him in a direction God didn't want Balaam to go. God literally spoke to Balaam through that donkey. "Then the LORD gave the donkey the ability to speak. 'What have I done to you that deserves your beating me three times?' it asked Balaam" (Numbers 22:28 NLT). Then God revealed that the donkey had seen the angel of the Lord blocking Balaam's path. By balking, that donkey had saved his errant master's life.

So why should it surprise us that God spoke to our twenty-first century Peter through a dog...and a dog tag? Amazing how God gets our attention! How is God speaking to you today?

In the past God spoke to our ancestors through the prophets at many times and in various ways, but in these last days he has spoken to us by his Son, whom he

appointed heir of all things, and through whom also he made the universe (Hebrews 1:1-2).

Consider This:

Recall the interesting, nontraditional creative ways God has used to get your attention. After your attention was gotten, were there any aha moments that followed? Have you ever shared these stories or epiphanies with others?

Puppy in a Haystack
God Restores

The church is the great lost and found department.
Robert Short

Early in their marriage, my friends Val and Jim got a female Beagle puppy they named Beazley. Their eldest son was a toddler then, and he and the pup were little together. Beazley weighed only about six pounds…small enough to get lost when her people weren't watching. And one day, she did.

Val had heard some noise outside and went to investigate. A small neighborhood parade was passing by. She stood watching from her front porch. She never noticed the puppy slip past her and wander away.

Not until later did the family realize their dog was gone. Val's little boy was devastated. Val was too. She feared Beazley might be lost to them forever. The tiny pup had not been wearing any kind of identification. She and Jim worked for an urban ministry and some female ministry staff shared a house half a mile away. But, apart from them, she didn't really know her neighbors.

Val called the staff women and asked for prayer. She prayed all afternoon—while her little boy wept. At about 4 p.m., the phone rang. Unbelievably, one of the staff women had seen Beazley near her own home. She had caught the pup and brought her inside. Val went to fetch her and Beazley was home before dinner.

Then and now, Val believes finding Beazley was a miracle. There was a huge park between their home and the staff's house. Streets changed direction. What were the odds of this tiny puppy winding up in the only place where she would be recognized? But God is bigger than any odds or any problem and He reunited this wonderful dog with her people. Beazley grew to be 25 pounds, lived to a ripe old doggie age, and blessed her family all of her life.

Like Val, I lost something of value that God miraculously restored. One day last year I was taking a walk, glanced down, and saw that the ring I'd been wearing was missing its small emerald.

I had no idea where I'd lost it. I had been many places that day, and had washed my hands with the ring on. But I knew that God could restore that stone. I'd seen Him do this with a friend's diamond in response to prayer. I'd been speaking with a Bible study pal on my cell phone as I walked, and now we asked God to bring back my emerald if it was His will.

I was in the midst of a home remodel at the time. My contractor checked the traps beneath some sinks for me. No emerald. Two weeks passed, and I figured the jewel was lost forever.

One day I was out shopping for new kitchen appliances for the remodel. My cell phone rang. It was my contractor—calling with amazing news. A worker helping to install a glass door on a shower in one of my bathrooms had found my emerald on the tub's drain. I was in shock. I'd used that tub since the emerald had gone missing. By all accounts, that stone should have been long gone. But there it was! God had not only restored my treasure but multiplied my faith—and my contractor's faith as well!

Jesus's disciples thought they had lost a treasure too—one more precious by far than a dog or a jewel. They thought they'd lost their beloved Lord Jesus to death. They didn't fully understand what He had taught them. They didn't quite believe He would be raised from the dead. Even when His body went missing from the tomb, some thought it had simply been moved.

Mary Magdalene was one of those. When a pair of angels appeared to her and asked why she was crying, she told them, "They have taken my Lord away, and I don't know where they have put him" (John 20:13). But she and Jesus's other disciples soon learned that God had miraculously restored His Son, their Messiah—and through Him, would do the same for all who trusted Him for their salvation.

Precious as Beasley was to her people, glad as I was to get my jewel back, the greater treasure was seeing God at work. I am so grateful my God is a God of restoration. And I am grateful that through Christ's death, all those who would be lost to sin and death are "found" to spend eternity with Him.

For the Son of Man came to seek and to save the lost (Luke 19:10).

Consider This:

Have you ever lost a treasure (pet, object, person) that God restored? How did He do it? How has it affected your faith? How can you pray for restoration in your own and others' lives?

Dog Tails...er, Tales...by Author

M.R. Wells

Kris Young

Connie Fleishauer

Meet the Authors

M.R. Wells has written extensively for children's television and video programming, including several Disney shows, the animated PBS series *Adventures from The Book of Virtues*, and the action video series *Bibleman*. She shares her Southern California home with the kitties and puppies she adores: Muffin, Bo, Munchie, Becca, and Marley.

Kris Young has worked as a screenwriter for more than 20 years and currently teaches screenwriting at the LA Film Studies Center and UCLA. He lives in Southern California with his wife, Celine, and son, Skye.

Connie Fleishauer is a teacher and writer and enjoys filmmaking. She is also trained in voice-over work. She is the wife of a California farmer, a mother of three, a mother-in-law of two, and a grandma of one. Currently she and her husband care for Stuart, a Welsh corgi, and Squitchey, a little rescued dog.

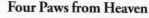

Four Paws from Heaven

Animal lovers will celebrate this pack of short dog tales and human stories. The enjoyable devotions provide entertaining and valuable lessons of faith, loyalty, and joy gleaned while walking through life alongside four paws.

Paws for Reflection

More than 50 humorous, poignant, and spiritually insightful stories are packed together under themed sections, including "Paws for Love: Curl Up with the Master." This gathering of short devotions reveals the faithfulness and companionship we get from canines and shares related insights for getting the most out of life.

Purr-ables from Heaven

Cats are quirky, but we adore them anyway—perhaps because they're a lot like us. This delightful book of devotions illustrates how even the most contradictory creatures can thrive in the presence of a loving, ever-patient owner. Each humorous and encouraging tale inspires us to delight in the Lord and lap up His loving presence.

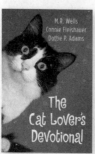

The Cat Lover's Devotional

Cat lovers will find inspirational stories of feline devotion, antics, and quirks in this warmhearted devotional. Each reading highlights cat behaviors that reflect God's heart. Readers will discover powerful insights on relationships, adoption, love, and patience as they open their hearts to the unique felines God blesses people with.

To learn more about books by M.R. Wells,
Kris Young, and Connie Fleishauer,
or to read sample chapters,
visit www.fourpawsfromheaven.com
or log on to our website:

www.harvesthousepublishers.com

HARVEST HOUSE PUBLISHERS

EUGENE, OREGON